Frommer's

Portland
day BY day®

3rd Edition

Portland
Oregon
OLD TOWN

by Donald Olson

Contents

Published by:

Frommer Media LLC

Copyright © 2018 Frommer Media LLC. All rights reserved. No part of this publication may be reproduced, stored in a retrieval system or transmitted in any form or by any means, electronic, mechanical, photocopying, recording, scanning or otherwise, except as permitted under Sections 107 or 108 of the 1976 United States Copyright Act, without the prior written permission of the Publisher. Requests to the Publisher for permission should be addressed to Support@FrommerMedia.com.

Frommer's is a trademark or registered trademark of Arthur Frommer.

ISBN: 978-1-628-87384-9 (paper); ISBN 978-1-628-87385-6 (ebk)

Editorial Director: Pauline Frommer
Editor: David Low
Production Editor: Heather Wilcox
Photo Editor: Meghan Lamb
Cartographer: Roberta Stockwell
Compositor: Lissa Auciello-Brogan
Indexer: Maro Riofrancos

Front cover photos, left to right: White Stag sign, Burnside Bridge, © Zenfolio.com. Portland sunrise view, Pittock Mansion, © Josemaria Toscano/Shuttercock.com. All the Apparatus band, Pioneer Courthouse Square, © Torsten Kjellstrand/Zenfolio.com

Back cover photo: Portland cable car view, © EQRoy/Shuttersstock.com

For information on our other products and services, please go to Frommers.com.

Frommer's also publishes its books in a variety of electronic formats. Some content that appears in print may not be available in electronic formats.

Manufactured in China

5 4 3 2 1

About this Guide

Organizing your time. That's what this guide is all about.

Other guides give you long lists of things to see and do and then expect you to fit the pieces together. The Day by Day guides are different. These guides tell you the best of everything, and then they show you how to see it *in the smartest, most time-efficient way*. Our authors have designed detailed itineraries organized by time, neighborhood, or special interest. And each tour comes with a bulleted map that takes you from stop to stop.

Planning a first-time trip to Portland with the kids? Looking for great ways to explore the Rose City by bike? Or maybe you want to know how to get the most out of the city even on a rainy Pacific Northwest day. Whatever your interest or schedule, the Day by Days give you the smartest routes to follow. Not only do we take you to the top attractions, hotels, and restaurants, but we also help you access those special moments that locals get to experience—those "finds" that turn tourists into travelers.

The Day by Days are also your top choice if you're looking for one complete guide for all your travel needs. The best hotels and restaurants for every budget, the greatest shopping values, the wildest nightlife—it's all here.

Why should you trust our judgment? Because our authors personally visit each place they write about. They're an independent lot who say what they think and would never include places they wouldn't recommend to their best friends. They're also open to suggestions from readers. If you'd like to contact them, please send your comments our way at Support@FrommerMedia.com, and we'll pass them on.

Enjoy your Day by Day guide—the most helpful travel companion you can buy. And have the trip of a lifetime.

About the Author

Donald Olson is a travel writer, novelist, and playwright. His travel stories have appeared in the *New York Times, National Geographic,* and other national publications. His travel guides for Frommer's include *Seattle Day by Day; Seattle, Portland & the Oregon Coast;* and *Berlin Day by Day.* His book *The Pacific Northwest Garden Tour* was named by *Library Journal* as one of the best reference books of 2014. His latest book, *The California Garden Tour,* was published by Timber Press in 2017.

Advisory & Disclaimer

Travel information can change quickly and unexpectedly, and we strongly advise you to confirm important details locally before traveling, including information on visas, health and safety, traffic and transport, accommodations, shopping, and eating out. We also encourage you to stay alert while traveling and to remain aware of your surroundings. Avoid civil disturbances, and keep a close eye on cameras, purses, wallets, and other valuables.

While we have endeavored to ensure that the information contained within this guide is accurate and up-to-date at the time of publication, we make no representations or warranties with respect to the accuracy or completeness of the contents of this work and specifically disclaim all warranties, including without limitation warranties of fitness for a particular purpose. We accept no responsibility or liability for any inaccuracy or errors or omissions, or for any inconvenience, loss, damage, costs, or expenses of any nature whatsoever incurred or suffered by anyone as a result of any advice or information contained in this guide.

The inclusion of a company, organization, or website in this guide as a service provider and/or potential source of further information does not mean that we endorse them or the information they provide. Be aware that information provided through some websites may be unreliable and can change without notice. Neither the publisher nor author shall be liable for any damages arising herefrom.

Star Ratings & Icons

Every hotel, restaurant, and attraction listing in this guide has been ranked for quality, value, service, amenities, and special features using a **star-rating system.** Hotels, restaurants, attractions, shopping, and nightlife are rated on a scale of zero stars (recommended) to three stars (exceptional). In addition to the star-rating system, we also use a **kids icon** to point out the best bets for families. Within each tour, we recommend cafes, bars, or restaurants where you can take a break. Each of these stops appears in a shaded box marked with a coffee-cup-shaped bullet ☕.

Frommers.com

Now that you have this guidebook to help you plan a great trip, visit our website at **www.frommers.com** for additional travel information on more than 4,000 destinations. We update features regularly to give you instant access to the most current trip-planning information available. At Frommers.com, you'll find scoops on the best airfares, lodging rates, and car rental bargains. You can even book your travel online through our reliable travel booking partners. Other popular features include:

- Online updates of our most popular guidebooks
- Vacation sweepstakes and contest giveaways
- Newsletters highlighting the hottest travel trends
- Podcasts, interactive maps, and up-to-the-minute event listings
- Opinionated blog entries by Arthur Frommer himself
- Online travel message boards with featured travel discussions

A Note on Prices

In the "Take a Break" (coffee-cup icon) and "Best Bets" sections of this book, we have used a system of dollar signs to show a range of costs for 1 night in a hotel (the price of a double-occupancy room) or the cost of an entree at a restaurant. Use the following table to decipher the dollar signs:

Cost	Hotels	Restaurants
$	under $125	under $15
$$	$125–$225	$15–$20
$$$	$225–$325	$20–$30
$$$$	$325–$400	$30–$40
$$$$$	over $400	over $40

How to Contact Us

In researching this book, we discovered many wonderful places—hotels, restaurants, shops, and more. We're sure you'll find others. Please tell us about them, so we can share the information with your fellow travelers in upcoming editions. If you were disappointed with a recommendation, we'd love to know that, too. Please write to: Support@FrommerMedia.com

16 Favorite Moments

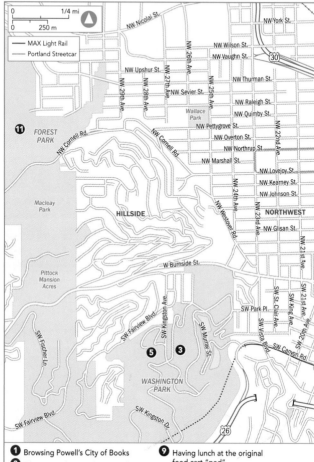

0 _____ 1/4 mi
0 _____ 250 m

— MAX Light Rail
— Portland Streetcar

NW Nicolai St.
NW York St.
NW Wilson St.
NW Vaughn St.
NW Thurman St.
NW Upshur St.
NW Sevier St.
NW Raleigh St.
NW Quimby St.
Wallace Park
NW Pettygrove St.
NW Overton St.
NW Northrup St.
NW Marshall St.
NW Lovejoy St.
NW Kearney St.
NW Johnson St.
NW Glisan St.

NW 29th Ave.
NW 28th Ave.
NW 27th Ave.
NW 26th Ave.
NW 25th Ave.
NW 24th Ave.
NW 23rd Ave.
NW 22nd Ave.
NW 21st Ave.

(30)

11 FOREST PARK

NW Cornell Rd.

Macleay Park

HILLSIDE

NW Westover Rd.

NORTHWEST

Pittock Mansion Acres

W Burnside St.

SW Park Pl.
SW St. Clair Ave.
SW King Ave.
SW 21st Ave.
SW 20th Ave.
SW Vista Blvd.
SW Canyon Rd.

SW Fischer Ln.

SW Fairview Blvd.

SW Fairview Blvd.

SW Kingston Ave.

5   **3**

SW Murray St.

WASHINGTON PARK

SW Kingston Dr.

(26)

Previous page: Strolling through the Portland Japanese Garden.

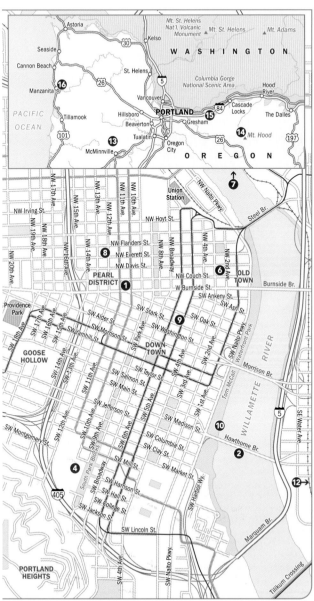

Sometimes Portland seems almost too good to be true. Just try to get locals to stop rhapsodizing about the cuisine, the live-ability and bike-ability, the great neighborhoods, the nearby mountains and ocean, the beer and wine and coffee and—see what I mean? Once the "undiscovered city" between San Francisco and Seattle, the City of Roses has now been discovered in a very big way, becoming a magnet for creative, outdoorsy folks young, old, and in-between—in short, for anyone who wants a vibrant, forward-thinking city that's also manageable. Popularity brings its own set of problems, of course, but let's accentuate the positive and have a look at just a few of the highlights.

Cycling across the Hawthorne Bridge.

1 Browsing Powell's City of Books. The world's top independent bookstore fills an entire city block (and that's just this branch) with over 1.5 million new and used books. It's pure bibliophile nirvana. *See p 78.*

2 Biking over the Hawthorne Bridge. Bicycling has long been a part of life in Portland, and with the city's new bike-share program biking has become more popular than ever. There's no better way to join the rolling masses than to take a spin across the historic Hawthorne Bridge over the Willamette River, especially in the evening. *See p 94.*

3 Gazing on Mount Hood from the International Rose Test Garden. The flowers are gorgeous and the views even better up in Washington Park. On a clear day, you can see multiple snowcapped peaks on the eastern horizon, with Mount Hood at center stage. *See p 90.*

4 Stocking up at the Portland State University Saturday Farmers Market. Local organic produce, baked goods, food carts, and

The International Rose Test Garden.

Saturday Farmers Market at Portland State University.

family-friendly entertainment make the Saturday-morning farmers market at PSU a Saturday must-do from March through December. *See p 82.*

⑤ Enjoying the superb land-scapes at the Portland Japanese Garden. The most authentic of its kind outside of Japan, the Portland Japanese Garden is a world-class destination that offers five meticulously created and maintained historic garden styles with new additions by famed Japanese architect Kengo Kuma. *See p 90.*

⑥ Venturing into the Shanghai Tunnels. For a peek into Portland's sordid past, when drunken sailors and drifters were "Shanghaied"— kidnapped and forced to work on oceangoing ships—take a guided underground tour. *See p 34.*

⑦ Heading over to Alberta Street for Last Thursdays. In the rest of the city, it's the first Thursday of every month that brings the gallery openings. Over on Alberta Street on the East Side, though, they go with the "Keep Portland Weird" theme and turn the whole street into one big party of art, music, and free-spirited independence on the *last* Thursday. *See p 22.*

⑧ Caffeinating at Caffe Umbria. In this City of Coffee, there are countless cafes to choose from; everyone has his or her favorite spot, and mine is Caffe Umbria, started by master coffee roasters from Perugia. Their bright, modern café in the Pearl District is the closest you'll come to an authentic Italian coffee and café experience. *See p 11.*

⑨ Having lunch at the original food cart "pod." On SW 5th Avenue between Oak and Stark streets, the line-up of food carts offers you a choice from a global variety of dishes including Cuban, Thai, Indian, pizza, or "Bulkogi Fusion" (that is, Korean tacos), to name just a few. *See p 110.*

⑩ Circumnavigating the Willamette River. One of my favorite Portland walks starts downtown in Governor Tom McCall Waterfront Park, crosses the Steel Bridge to the east side,

Lunch at the original food cart "pod."

Skiing on Mount Hood.

and continues along the Eastbank Esplanade, a floating walkway that offers a primo view of the downtown skyline. At the end of the esplanade, return downtown via the historic Hawthorne Bridge. *See p 93.*

⓫ **Rambling through Forest Park.** Eight square miles of wild forest, streams, gorges, and fern-covered hillsides wait on the west side of the city, just minutes from downtown, with more than 70 miles of hiking trails and fire roads to explore. *See p 86.*

⓬ **Catching a movie at the Bagdad Theater.** Order a microbrew and a slice of pizza and enjoy a second-run movie in this fully restored 1927 movie palace in the lively Hawthorne District. Stay for dinner or a drink afterward, or venture down the block for dozens of other nightlife options. *See p 129.*

⓭ **Tasting local pinot noirs in the Willamette Valley.** South of Portland, the mild climate and volcanic soil of the Willamette River Valley is ideal for growing wine grapes, which translates into more than 400 wineries. *See p 150.*

⓮ **Skiing on Mount Hood in the summer.** It's the only place in the country with lift-accessible skiing year-round, but it's even better in the winter. Or just head up to Mount Hood to enjoy the views from Timberline Lodge, a WPA masterpiece opened by FDR in 1938. *See p 142.*

⓯ **Hiking to a waterfall in the Columbia River Gorge.** There are plenty to choose from, but from the Oneonta Trailhead, one easy loop leads you to four waterfalls, including a cascade that you walk behind. Be forewarned, though: A wildfire in 2017 caused some road closures in and around the Gorge, so do a little research before you go. *See p 144.*

⓰ **Walking on an Oregon beach.** The Pacific Ocean is too chilly and wild up here to swim in, but Oregon's shoreline is spectacular and filled with towering headlands, white-sand beaches and charming beach towns you can reach on an easy day trip from Portland. *See p 155.* ●

Ponytail Falls in the Columbia River Gorge.

The Best in **One Day**

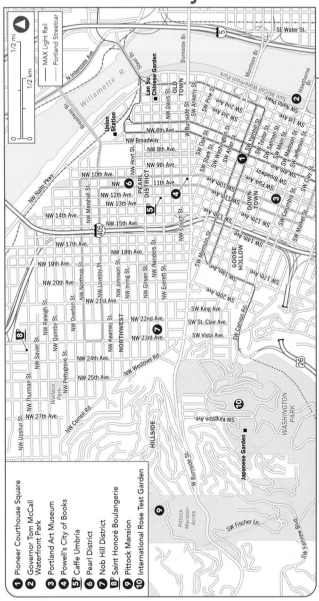

MAX Light Rail
Portland Streetcar

1/2 mi
1/2 km

1 Pioneer Courthouse Square
2 Governor Tom McCall Waterfront Park
3 Portland Art Museum
4 Powell's City of Books
5 Caffe Umbria
6 Pearl District
7 Nob Hill District
8 Saint Honoré Boulangerie
9 Pittock Mansion
10 International Rose Test Garden

Previous page: Giant tree samples at World Forestry Center Discovery Museum.

This full-day ramble starts in downtown Portland and ventures up into the West Hills, giving a great overview—literally—of the city's top offerings. After rambling along the riverfront, you'll probably want to trade your walking shoes for a streetcar or bus to reach the final few stops. START: **MAX to Pioneer Courthouse/SW 6th Ave. or Pioneer Square South. Bus: 1, 12, 19, or 94 to Pioneer Courthouse Square.**

❶ ★★★ Pioneer Courthouse Square. "Portland's living room" anchors downtown and embodies the Rose City in all its eclectic, endearing scruffiness, sophistication and charm. It's a place to people-watch and mingle, filled with shoppers, locals on lunch break, commuters arriving and departing on buses, streetcars, and the MAX light-rail, and everyone in between. You'll often find some kind of outdoor event going on, be it a farmer's market (Mon, June–Oct), Italian food festival, rock concert, or sand castle–building competition. An information center and a TriMet ticket office are available to visitors. The graceful cupola of the Pioneer Courthouse at the east end of the square has been a Portland landmark since 1875. ⏱ *15 min. Btw. SW 6th Ave., Broadway, Yamhill & Morrison sts.* ☎ *503/223-1613. www.thesquarepdx.org. Visitor center Mon–Fri 8:30am–5:30pm, Sat 10am–4pm. MAX: Pioneer Courthouse. Bus: 1, 12, 19, or 94.*

❷ ★★★ kids Governor Tom McCall Waterfront Park. What a different place Portland would be if this 1½-mile green swath along the west bank of the Willamette

Governor Tom McCall Waterfront Park during Portland's Rose Festival.

River was still a freeway, as it was in the past. Now it's one of the city's best places to stroll, bike, view Portland's historic bridges, or enjoy one of the many yearly festivals held here. In the hotter months, kids love cooling off in the Salmon Street Springs fountain at Salmon Street, with 185 computer-controlled water jets. The ever-popular **Saturday Market** (also held on Sun) is a long-standing crafts and food market beneath the Burnside Bridge, just past the 1947 sternwheeler that houses the **Oregon Maritime Center and Museum** (p 53). Farther down, the **Japanese American Historical Plaza** at Davis Street commemorates—with poetry-inscribed rocks and spring-flowering cherry trees—Oregon's Japanese-American citizens interned during World War II. 🕐 *1 hr. Naito Parkway btw. Steel Bridge & RiverPlace Marina. Open daily. MAX: Yamhill District, Oak/SW 1st Ave., or Old Town/Chinatown.*

❸ ★★ **Portland Art Museum.** Founded in 1892, the Northwest's oldest art museum is a one-stop overview of art from regional Native American artifacts to contemporary painting and photography. The permanent collection includes more than 5,000 objects by Northwest artists, a Rembrandt Peale portrait of George Washington, and van Gogh's *The Ox-Cart*. There's an outdoor sculpture garden and additional galleries in the adjacent building, a former Masonic temple. The art museum is also the home of the Northwest Film Center, which offers classes and shows classic, foreign, and independent works through the year in the Whitsell Auditorium. 🕐 *1½ hr. 1219 SW Park*

One of many rooms at the vast Powell's City of Books.

Ave. ☎ *503/226-2811. www.portland artmuseum.org. Admission $20 adults, $17 seniors, free for kids under 18, free for everyone 5–8pm the 4th Fri of the month. Tues, Wed, Sat & Sun 10am–5pm, Thurs–Fri 10am–8pm. Streetcar: Art Museum.*

❹ ★★★ **kids Powell's City of Books.** Few cities identify with a bookstore as closely as Portland does with Powell's, the world's largest—and many would say best—independent bookseller. Powell's downtown flagship store fills a full city block with over 1.5 million new and used books spread through nine color-coded rooms. You'll need a map, and probably a cup of coffee from the World Cup coffee shop, but you'll be rewarded with the ultimate bibliophile browsing experience. Powell's hosts regular free author readings (I've done a couple of them myself). Book collectors won't want to miss the Rare Books Room, full of signed first editions, plus a priceless 1814 account of Lewis and Clark's journey. ⏱ *1 hr. 1005 W. Burnside Ave.* ☎ *503/228-4651. www.powells.com. Daily 9am–11pm; Rare Book Room Sat–Sun 11am–7pm. Streetcar: NW Couch. Bus: 20.*

For an excellent cappuccino and maybe a panini sandwich or a gelato, head over to **5** **Caffè Umbria,** a sophisticated cafe/bar in the true Italian style. *303 NW 12th Ave.* ☎ *503/241-5300. www.caffe umbria.com. $.*

6 ★★ **kids Pearl District.** Continue your tour on foot, or hop on the Portland Streetcar NS line at NW Couch Street for a leisurely trip through the heart of Portland's most successful new neighborhood. Over the past couple of decades, this former industrial warehouse area has been transformed by a mix of condo and apartment buildings, art galleries, cafes, urban parks like **Jamison Square** (p 49) and **Tanner Springs Park** (p 49), small specialty stores, and restaurants galore. See p 48 for more details. ⏱ *1 hr. Bounded by W. Burnside St., NW Naito Pkwy., NW 14th Ave. & Broadway. Streetcar: NS line from NW Couch to NW 23rd Ave.*

7 ★★ **Nob Hill District.** Northwest Portland's walkable commercial district centers on two streets: NW 23rd Avenue, lined with shops, restaurants, and boutiques, and NW 21st Avenue, with more restaurants (the Portland Streetcar NS line stops at both streets). National retailers like Urban Outfitters, Rejuvenation Hardware, and Pottery Barn cluster at the south end of NW 23rd near Burnside. Head north for boutiques selling trendy clothes and accessories, locally made jewelry, and New Age books

Hanging out by the streetcar line in the Pearl District.

The Pittock Mansion's elegant music room.

Named after the patron saint of bakers, the cozy **8** **Saint Honoré Boulangerie** cafe and bakery serves French pastries and rustic breads fresh from the clay firebrick oven. Sit at a sidewalk table or take a seat at the communal table indoors, both good spots to linger over a hot or cold drink and a delicious pastry. *2335 NW Thurman St. (at 23rd Ave.).* ☎ *503/445-4342. www. sainthonorebakery.com. $.*

9 ★★★ **Pittock Mansion.** The home of Portland pioneer Henry Pittock—publisher of the *Oregonian* newspaper and part of the first party to climb Mt. Hood—looks out over the city from 1,000 feet above in the West Hills, at the edge of Forest Park. Built in 1914, the 23-room French Renaissance Revival chateau combines Northwest materials and workmanship with Turkish, French, and English design touches, along with newfangled (for its time) inventions like an

and paraphernalia as well as plenty of restaurant choices. Every block has somewhere to browse, nibble, or nosh. ⏱ *1½ hr. NW 23rd Ave. btw. Burnside & Thurman sts.; NW 21st Ave. btw. Burnside & Northrup sts. Streetcar: NW 23rd & Marshall. Bus: 15.*

The International Rose Test Garden.

Family Fun Pass

If you're traveling with kids and plan on making the rounds of the city's major sights, you can save money with the **Family Fun Pass** ($79). This is a private (not a city-sponsored) pass, but it covers several family-friendly attractions including the Oregon Zoo, Lan Su Chinese Garden, Oregon History Museum, Pittock Mansion, Oaks Park Roller Rink, and some smaller museums and attractions outside the city. The pass provides entrance to each attraction for up to four people. It's available online, spring and summer only, at www.familyfunpass.org.

intercom system and an elevator. The view from the front lawn, east across the city as far as Mt. Hood, is worth the trip in itself. You can hike here along the Wildwood Trail from Washington Park or Forest Park. *3229 NW Pittock Dr.* ☎ *503/823-3623. www.pittockmansion.org. Sept–Dec & Feb–May daily 11am–4pm, June–Aug daily 10am–5pm, closed Jan. Admission $10 adults, $9 seniors, $7 kids 6–18.*

⓾ ★★★ International Rose Test Garden. Portland's nickname, "The City of Roses," reaches an apogee high in the hills of Washington Park, where about 10,000 rosebushes thrive in the oldest continuously operating official rose-test garden in the United States. Founded in 1917, the garden follows its mission to test and preserve new rose hybrids, but

even the non-green-thumbed will love the combination of fragrant blooms and fantastic views. From the Miniature Rose Garden at the top, the roses fill tiered beds that descend a hillside blazing with color and scent. Look for a wall in the Shakespeare Garden, home to plants mentioned in the Bard's plays, where you'll find a fitting quote: "Of all flowers methinks a rose is best." (For more Washington Park attractions, see p 88.) ⏱ *30 min. In summer, go early in the morning or in the evening for smaller crowds. 400 SW Kingston Ave.* ☎ *503/823-3636. www.rosegardenstore.org. Daily 7:30am–9pm. Free admission. Free guided tours given June–Sept at 11:30am Tues & 1pm Sat & Sun. MAX: Washington Park Station. (In summer, a bus shuttle runs from the station to the gardens every 15 min.) Bus: 63.*

The Best in **Two Days**

1 Portland Japanese Garden
2 Oregon Zoo
3 South Park Blocks
4 Oregon Historical Society
5 Lan Su Chinese Garden
6 Tao of Tea Teahouse
7 Steel Bridge
8 Oregon Museum of Science and Industry
9 Hawthorne District
10 The Waffle Window

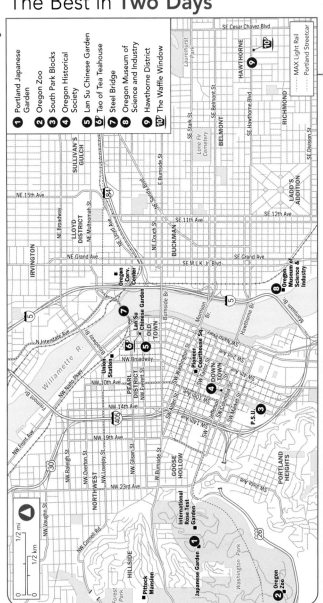

- - - - - MAX Light Rail
· · · · · · Portland Streetcar

If you have 2 days, follow the preceding tour for your first day, then start the second one in Washington Park. From there you'll head downhill and across the river to OMSI, ending up in Portland's liveliest southeast district. If you time it right, you'll finish the day with another hilltop sunset, this time from the top of Mt. Tabor. START: **Washington Park. MAX Oregon Zoo. Bus 63.**

❶ ★★★ **Portland Japanese Garden.** This serene masterpiece of Japanese-garden design opened in 1967 in the heart of Washington Park and offers five historic Japanese garden styles and a striking new entrance plaza, teahouse and buildings designed by renowned Japanese architect Kengo Kuma. Considered the finest example of its kind outside of Japan, the 5½-acre garden fits Portland's misty, moody climate perfectly and is beautiful in any season. A walking path winds from the entrance plaza through meticulously tended and interconnected landscapes that feature streams, gates, rocks, lanterns, a zig-zag bridge, a koi pond and waterfall, and two dry gardens with rocks and carefully raked patterns

in sand and stone. Traditional and seasonal events and exhibits, including theater and music performances and autumn moon viewing, take place throughout the year. (For more Washington Park attractions, see p 88.) ⏱ *1 hr. 611 SW Kingston Ave.* ☎ *503/223-1321. www.japanesegarden.com. Admission $15 adults, $13 seniors & college students, $11 kids 6–17. Mar–Sept Mon noon–7pm, Tues–Sun 10am–7pm; Oct–Mar Mon noon–4pm, Tues–Sun 10am–4pm. Free guided tours noon daily Mar–Oct; Sat & Sun only Nov–Mar. MAX: Washington Park; free bus shuttle to garden in summer. Bus: 63 (weekdays only).*

❷ ★★★ **kids Oregon Zoo.** The state's top tourist attraction, the zoo is best known for its elephants,

The koi pond at the Portland Japanese Garden.

A polar bear frolics at the Oregon Zoo.

the most successful breeding herd in captivity. The Africa exhibit is one of the best habitats with a manmade rainforest and a savanna populated by zebras, rhinos, giraffes, and hippos. The Alaskan Tundra has grizzly bears, wolves, and musk oxen, while the Cascade Crest exhibit features a mountain goat habitat. In Steller Cove, Steller sea lions and sea otters are on display. Other exhibits include an intriguing bat house and the Amazon Flooded Forest. In the summer, there are outdoor concerts in the zoo's amphitheater. A much-loved miniature train pulled by a real steam engine puffs around the zoo and on a 4-mile loop to the International Rose Test Garden and Portland Japanese Garden. ⏱ *2 hr. 4001 SW Canyon Rd.* ☎ *503/226-1561. www.oregonzoo.org. Admission (seasonally adjusted) $10–$15 adults, $8–$13 seniors, $5–$10 children 3–11. Late May to early Sept daily 9:30am–6pm; early Sept to May daily 9:30am–4pm; Jan–Feb daily 10am–4pm. MAX: Washington Park. Bus: 63 (weekdays only).*

❸ ★ **South Park Blocks.** Portland's first parks, set aside in 1852, are still a peaceful respite in the heart of downtown. Stately oaks, elms, and maples shade 12 grassy blocks between SW Salmon and SW Jackson streets. Public art on every block ranges from the heroic (statues of Teddy Roosevelt and Lincoln) to the abstract (three granite blocks titled "Peace Chant"). The southern end, part of Portland State University, is closed to car traffic and home to the Portland Farmers Market (see p 45) on Saturday mornings from spring through fall. ⏱ *30 min. Open daily.*

❹ ★★ **Oregon Historical Society.** Delve into the past of Oregon and the entire Pacific Northwest at this museum run by the Oregon Historical Society on the South Park Blocks. As a repository of artifacts relating to Oregon history, it is unsurpassed. The main permanent exhibit is the award-winning "Oregon My Oregon," which takes up an entire floor and includes a 9,000-year-old sagebrush sandal and the lunch counter from

Newberry's, a famous downtown eatery. Other exhibits, permanent and traveling, cover topics such as Lewis and Clark, the Oregon Trail, western Native baskets, and Portland's major league soccer team, the Timbers. ⏱ *30 min. 1200 SW Park Ave.* ☎ *503/306-5198. www. ohs.org. Admission $11 adults, $9 seniors/students, $5 children 6–18. Mon–Sat 10am–5pm, Sun noon–5pm. MAX: SW 6th & Madison sts. Street-car: Art Museum. Bus: 6, 38, 43, 45, 55, 58, 68, 92, or 96.*

❺ ★★★ **Lan Su Chinese Garden.** This remarkable gem hidden in Portland's Chinatown is a Ming Dynasty–style classical Chinese garden complete with lake, bridges, elaborate pavilions, and a two-story teahouse. All the wooden buildings, decorative windows, and 500 tons of decorative rock were shipped from Suzhou, China, and reassembled by a team of craftspeople, also from Suzhou, in 2000. Every season highlights the carefully planned landscape and plantings in a different way, from spring blooms and fall leaves to the bare branches of winter and the lush flowers and scents of summer. Both fascinating and surprising, it's considered the most authentic urban Chinese garden outside of China. ⏱ *45 min. Entrance at NW 3rd Ave. & Everett St. www.lansu garden.org. Admission $10 adults, $9 seniors, $7 students & kids 6–18. Free tours hourly btw. 11am–2pm (call to verify times). Apr–Oct daily 10am–6pm; Nov–Mar daily 10am–5pm. MAX: Old Town Chinatown. Bus: 4, 8, 9, 16, 35, 44, or 77.*

What better way to recharge than over a cup of oolong at ❻ **Tao of Tea Teahouse** inside the Tower of Cosmic Reflections, gazing over Lake Zither in the Lan Su Chinese Garden? Along with a huge selection of teas, the teahouse offers a short list of sweets and nibbles. ☎ *503/224-8455. $.*

A sunny day at the Portland Farmers Market.

The iconic Steel Bridge crosses the Willamette River.

❼ ★★ Steel Bridge. Of all Portland's bridges, this 210-foot span, built in 1912, offers the most ways to cross the Willamette River. The upper deck carries cars and MAX light rail, while the lower accommodates trains, cyclists, and pedestrians, the latter two on a cantilevered walkway that connects Waterfront Park to the Vera Katz Eastbank Esplanade. Bridge buffs ahoy: It's the world's only double-deck vertical lift bridge whose lower deck can lift independently of the upper one. It's the second-oldest vertical lift bridge in North America. (Hawthorne Bridge—also in Portland—is the oldest.) ⏱ *15 min. Btw. NW Naito Pkwy./NW Glisan St. & N Interstate Ave./NE Multnomah St.*

❽ ★★ kids Oregon Museum of Science and Industry. Set, fittingly, in a former power plant on the east bank of the Willamette River, OMSI is all about engaging with science, offering dozens of hands-on exhibits, games, brain teasers, and all the technology you could wish for. Earth Hall features exhibits on environmental hazards, natural disasters, and climate change. Life Hall deals with the mysteries of human growth and development. Science Labs is a hands-on laboratory experience in chemistry, physics, and technology. The Turbine Hall, devoted to the physical sciences and technology, lets visitors build an aqueduct and program a robot. Three additional components require separate tickets: **the Empirical Theater** (formerly called the OMNIMAX), the **Kendall Planetarium,** which features astronomy and laser-light shows, and the **USS** *Blueback* **submarine** docked in the river right behind the museum. ⏱ *1½ hr. 1945 SE Water Ave. ☎ 503/797-4000. www.omsi.edu. Museum $14 adults, $11 seniors, $9.75 children 3–13; Empirical Theater shows $7–$8.50 adults, $6.50 seniors & children 3–13; submarine tours $6.75 all ages; planetarium shows $5.75–$7.50; discounted combination tickets available. Mid-June to early Sept daily 9:30am–7pm; early Sept to mid-June Tues–Sun 9:30am–5pm. Bus: 4, 6, 10, 14, 31, 32, or 33. Streetcar: OMSI.*

❾ ★★ Hawthorne District. Portland's longtime epicenter of eclecticism stretches along

Travel Tip

How about a vacation from driving? Portland's extensive interconnected system of buses, streetcars, and light-rail trains (MAX) lets you do just that. It's all operated by Tri-Met—go to **www.trimet.org** for a handy set of easy-to-use navigational tools to help you plan your trip from point A to B. (For streetcar information go to **www.portlandstreetcar.org**). MAX and streetcar routes operate on an honor system; buy your tickets before you board at vending machines at every stop. Buses require a ticket, a pass, or exact change. See p 166 for more information on Portland's public transportation and money-saving options for getting around town.

Hawthorne Boulevard between 30th and 42nd avenues, packed with restaurants, cafes, bars, boutiques, thrift stores, and theaters. Most of the action is concentrated between 34th and 39th avenues, including the historic Bagdad Theater & Pub (see p 129) and a branch of Powell's Books. It's an easily walkable stretch, with plenty of options for shopping and noshing. See p 63 for more details. ⏱ *1 hr.* Bus: 14.

If you still think waffles are just for breakfast, peek around the corner from the Bread and Ink Café for 🔟 **The Waffle Window** and step up to order creative concoctions like the Three Bs (brie, basil, and pepper bacon). They also offer classic waffle toppings like berries, jam, and syrup. On nice days, you can sit outside at the picnic tables. *3610 SE Hawthorne Blvd.* ☎ *503/239-4756.* *www.wafflewindow.com. $.*

A screening at the Empirical Theater, Oregon Museum of Science and Industry.

The Best in **Three Days**

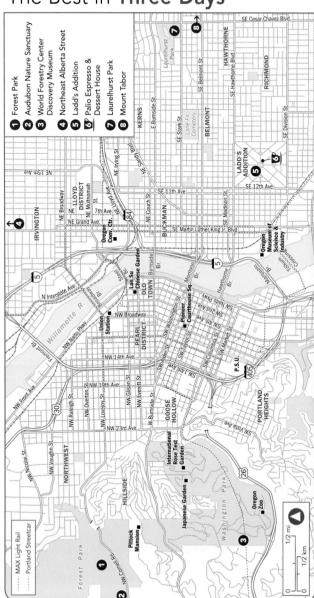

1 Forest Park
2 Audubon Nature Sanctuary
3 World Forestry Center Discovery Museum
4 Northeast Alberta Street
5 Ladd's Addition
6 Palio Espresso & Dessert House
7 Laurelhurst Park
8 Mount Tabor

MAX Light Rail
Portland Streetcar

0   1/2 mi
0   1/2 km

Having 3 days to play with lets you venture farther afield and explore Portland in greater depth. The itinerary begins in the largest urban forest in North America, heads over to always-fascinating Washington Park, and zips across the Willamette to visit the vibrantly revitalized Alberta Street neighborhood in the northeast and two charming and leafy old southeast neighborhoods, Ladd's Addition and Laurelhurst. You'll end your third day atop an extinct volcano called Mt. Tabor. START: **Bus 15 to NW Thurman & 29th Ave. (Lower MacLeay Park).**

❶ ★★★ Forest Park. Portland's leafy backyard (or front yard, depending on where you live) covers 8 square miles of the West Hills, making it the country's largest urban forest reserve. (It's over six times the size of New York's Central Park and serves as a wildlife corridor for animals ranging from bobcats (rare), coyotes, and black-tailed deer to pygmy owls and woodpeckers. Small streams and over 70 miles of trails wind through the park's forested hillsides and valleys, including the popular 30-mile **Wildwood Trail,** a National Recreation Trail. (Mountain bikers are limited to access roads and fire lanes.) It's also amazingly close to downtown; the **Lower MacLeay Park** trailhead at the end of NW Upshur Street is easy to access on foot, and NW Thurman Street turns into **Leif Ericson Drive,** the park's main travel artery. From there you can hike to the **Pittock Mansion** (p 90), **Washington Park** (p 88), or go as far as Gresham on the 40-Mile Loop from the Wildwood Trail. See p 86 for more details on Forest Park's recreation options. ⏱ *1½ hr. Numerous trail heads.* ☎ *503/823-7529. www.forestpark conservancy.org. Open daily. Dogs must be leashed. Bus: 15, 20.*

Joggers in Forest Park.

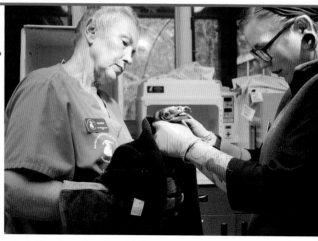

The Audubon Nature Sanctuary's Wildlife Care Center.

2 kids ★ **Audubon Nature Sanctuary.** For a quick taste of Portland's lush city-edge forests, with a close-up animal encounter or two thrown in for free, head to this 150-acre public reserve at Forest Park's southern end. Four miles of trails lead along Balch Creek and under old-growth Douglas firs, and from here you can access the Wildwood and Upper MacLeay trails in Forest Park proper. The **Wildlife Care Center** is Oregon's oldest and most active, giving thousands of injured animals per year another chance at life in the wild. You never know who'll be in residence: Beavers, bald eagles, great horned owls, and turtles have all made appearances. ⏱ *1 hr. 5151 NW Cornell Rd.* ☎ *503/292-6855. www.audubonportland.org/sanctuaries. Open daily, trails dawn to dusk, care center 9am–5pm. Free admission. Bus: 15 (plus 1½-mile walk from NW 23rd & Lovejoy St.).*

3 ★ kids **World Forestry Center Discovery Museum.** Oregon's economy was founded on logging, and the timber industry, continues to play an important role in the state. This museum attempts to explain how forests work and how complex they are. Exhibits on the first floor concentrate on the vast forests of the Pacific Northwest; those on the second floor focus on Russia, China, South Africa, and the Amazon. Keep in mind that no matter how "sustainable" their practices, the timber industry is about harvesting forests, not letting them be. ⏱ *45 min. 4033 SW Canyon Rd.* ☎ *503/228-1367. www.worldforestry.org. Admission $7 adults, $6 seniors, $5 kids 3–18. Daily 10am–5pm. MAX: Washington Park. Bus: 63.*

4 ★★ **Northeast Alberta Street.** From here, you have several options for how to spend the rest of your day. Looking for a case study in gentrification with a high hipster factor? Northeast Alberta Street between 15th and 33rd avenues is one of the more interesting neighborhoods on Portland's east side. The main drag is chock-full of restaurants, shops, theaters, and art galleries; see p 58 for more details. Most businesses throw their doors open on the last Thursday of every month for the city's funkiest monthly street fair, complete with music, clowns, and carefully balanced "tall bikes." ⏱ 1 hr. *NE Alberta St. btw. 15th & 33rd aves.*

⑤ ★★ Ladd's Addition. Or perhaps you'd prefer this designated historic district, great for a shady stroll under the magnificent old elm trees that line the streets. Created by and named for William Ladd, a 19th-century mayor who had a farm here (he owned most of today's east side of Portland), Ladd's Addition—one of Portland's oldest planned residential districts—breaks up the east side's neat street grid into an 8-by-10-block division of diagonals and roundabouts unlike any other neighborhood on the West Coast. The neighborhood's odd road alignments leave room for four diamond-shaped gardens, each overflowing in season with roses (of course), as well as a larger circular park inside the central roundabout. ⏱ 1 hr. *Btw. SE Hawthorne St., Division St., 12th Ave. & 20th Ave. Bus: 4, 10, 14, or 70.*

Rest your feet and enjoy a Mexican Mocha or a slice of key lime pie at **⑥ Palio Espresso & Dessert House,** a cozily romantic coffee shop and cafe right across the street from the neighborhood's central garden. Stumptown coffee and plenty of different teas are served in a setting that feels a bit like an antique bookstore. *1996 SE Ladd Ave.* ☎ *503/232-9412.* $.

⑦ ★★ kids Laurelhurst Park. In the mood for more park rambling? Thank former mayor William Ladd (see Ladd's Addition, above) and the famous Olmsted Brothers landscape design firm for this 26-acre park in the neighborhood of the same name (Laurelhurst). Grand old trees shade paved trails, picnic tables, and open lawns,

Smoke jumper simulator in the World Forestry Center Discovery Museum.

PDX Playlist

Seattle and L.A. may get more press, but Portland has been home to outstanding live music ever since The Kingsmen garbled their way through "Louie, Louie" in one take in 1963. (After a 2-year obscenity investigation, the FBI concluded the song was "unintelligible at any speed.") Here's the perfect soundtrack of local, or at least once-local, artists for your visit:

- "Louie, Louie," The Kingsmen, 1963
- "I Can't Wait," Nu Shooz, *Poolside*, 1986
- "Ride," Dandy Warhols, *Dandys Rule, OK?* 1995
- "I Will Buy You a New Life," Everclear, *So Much for the Afterglow*, 1997
- "Between the Bars," Elliott Smith, *Either/Or*, 1997
- "Light Rail Coyote," Sleater-Kinney, *One Beat*, 2002
- "Phantom Limb," The Shins, *Chutes Too Narrow*, 2003
- "Let's Never Stop Falling in Love," Pink Martini, *Hang On Little Tomato*, 2004
- "On the Bus Mall," The Decemberists, *Picaresque*, 2005
- "People Say," Portugal. The Man, *The Satanic Satanist*, 200

including an off-leash area for dogs; it is most definitely one of the city's prettiest parks. Originally a spring-fed pond, 3-acre Firwood Lake was dredged in 2011 and fitted with a water circulation and aeration system. The lawn next to it is the best spot on the east side to lounge away a sunny Friday afternoon. A smaller "play park" section between SE Oak and Stark streets has tennis courts, a soccer field, a playground, bathrooms, and a small dance studio for public recreation classes. ⏱ *45 min. Btw. SE 33rd & 39th aves., Oak & Ankeny sts. Daily 5am–10:30pm. Bus: 75.*

❽ ★★ Mount Tabor. If you're eager for more urban but outdoorsy action, venture out to this 190-acre city park. How many cities in the continental U.S. can boast an extinct volcano within their city limits? Only two, actually, and they're both in Oregon: Bend and Portland. The 630-foot-high cinder cone of Portland's Mount Tabor is topped by three open reservoirs (recently disconnected from the water system but still used as a "water feature"). Its forests are laced with trails for bikers and hikers, and near a large playground, an amphitheater hosts free outdoor concerts on Tuesday evenings in the summer. ⏱ *1 hr. Daily 5am–10pm, closed to motor vehicles Wed. Enter at SE Salmon St. & 60th Ave., SE Lincoln & 64th Ave., SE Yamhill & 69th Ave., or SE Harrison St. & 71st Ave. Bus: 4, 15, or 71.* ●

Portland with Kids

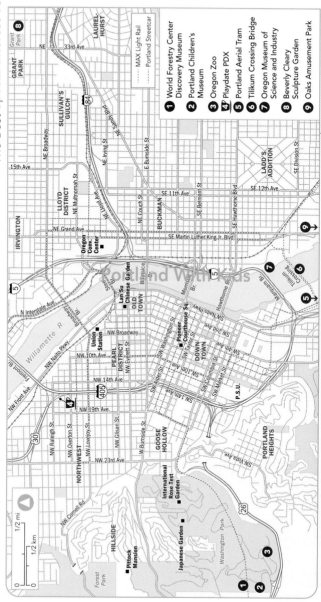

1 World Forestry Center Discovery Museum
2 Portland Children's Museum
3 Oregon Zoo
4 Playdate PDX
5 Portland Aerial Tram
6 Tilikum Crossing Bridge
7 Oregon Museum of Science and Industry
8 Beverly Cleary Sculpture Garden
9 Oaks Amusement Park

Previous page: The Portland Aerial Tram.

Portland repeatedly gets voted one of the best cities in the country to raise kids. It has a multitude of family-friendly and family-oriented places to experience, but kids are pretty much welcomed everywhere without much fuss or attitude. Portland is an active city, too, with a sense of outdoor adventure. Kids love the bridges, the river, the hiking trails, biking, skating, riding the light-rail and streetcars, and visiting Washington Park. For bigger adventures that the entire family can enjoy, don't forget the spectacular beaches, headlands, and lighthouses along the Oregon coast, just a couple of hours away (see p 154). START: **MAX to Washington Park. Bus 63 on weekdays.**

A canopy lift ride at the World Forestry Center Discovery Museum.

❶ ★ **World Forestry Center Discovery Museum.** At this paean to all things arboreal, kids especially love the virtual smoke-jumper and river-rafting exhibits—and after a visit here they'll be ready to dive into the real forests of Washington Park right outside. *See p 22,* ❸.

❷ ★★ **Portland Children's Museum.** Right next door is a castle of creativity and fun, one of the oldest of its kind in the country. The displays are constantly updated—and hands-on, of course—including exhibits themed around popular characters like Curious George and Clifford the Big

Fun at the Portland Children's Museum.

Outdoor Fountains

In the heat of the summer, the irony of cavorting in water in such a damp city evaporates like puddles on concrete, and kids pack Portland's many public water fountains. Even if it's too cool or cloudy to splash, the fountains are still fun to see. Just don't take a drink; they all use chlorinated, recycled water. Fountains generally flow from spring through fall. The city has many year-round indoor and summer-only outdoor pools. You'll find a listing of all of them at www.travelportland.com.

- **Ira Keller Fountain.** If you can't make it up the Columbia Gorge, this fountain in the heart of downtown is the closest you'll come to a waterfall: an abstract rock face of edges and drop-offs spilling 75,000 gallons of water. Too steep and slippery for climbing, this fountain is more for visual enjoyment and wading. *SW 3rd Ave. & SW Clay St.*

- **Jamison Square Fountain.** One of Portland's most popular hot-weather destinations fills a block in the Pearl District. The shallow wading pool is geared toward toddlers and babies, while older kids can clamber up the steps of the cascades. The other half of the park consists of grass and trees for lounging in the shade. *NW 11th Ave. & Johnson St.*

- **Salmon Street Springs.** The most distinctive and impressive of the city's fountains anchors the southern end of Governor Tom McCall Waterfront Park. Concentric circles of 185 jets spout water in every imaginable pattern, controlled by an underground computer that changes the pattern every 20 minutes. Almost 5,000 gallons of water a minute gush at peak volume—so older toddlers, grade-schoolers, and pre-teens will enjoy it most. *SW Naito Pkwy. & SW Salmon St. in Governor Tom McCall Waterfront Park.*

- **Teachers Fountain.** The newest public square downtown, dedicated to educators, has a gentle fountain with low jets and burbles feeding into a shallow pool ringed by benches. *SW Yamhill & SW Park aves.*

Red Dog. Kids age 10 and under can burrow in the rubber gravel of the Dig Pit, sculpt a city in the Clay Studio, build something in the Garage, or take the stage at the Play It Again Theater. A stop at the Water Works will probably require a change of clothes, but it's worth it. The Baby's Garden caters to tots under 3. A varying schedule of classes and story times keeps things fresh. **Note:** The museum can get crowded at peak times, so consider coming on weekday late

Up close with a parrot at the Oregon Zoo.

At **4** **Playdate PDX**'s 7,500-square-foot indoor playground, you can enjoy a panini and coffee while your progeny run wild on a multi-story castle with ropes, swings, and slides. Admission isn't cheap—$8 to $14 per kid, $4 to $8 ages 3 and under—and it can get packed; but on a rainy day it's a real stress-reducer. *1434 NW 17th Ave.* ☎ *503/227-7529. www.playdate pdx.com. Sun–Thurs 9am–8pm, Fri–Sat 9am–9pm. $.*

afternoons, when school groups have left. ⏱ *1½ hr. 4015 SW Canyon Rd.* ☎ *503/223-6500. www. portlandcm.org. $11 adults & children, $9.75 seniors, free for children under age 1 (free for all on first Fri of each month 4–8pm). Daily 9am–5pm. MAX: Washington Park. Bus: 63 on weekdays only.*

3 ★★★ **Oregon Zoo.** It's hard to decide which animals children like best here: the frolicking river otters, the powerful Amur tigers, the acrobatic chimpanzees, or the naked mole rats. In any case, the miniature train is a sure-fire favorite, circling the zoo and venturing off into the rest of Washington Park. Come early or stay late to increase your odds of seeing animals in action. *See p 15,* **2**.

5 ★ **Portland Aerial Tram.** A fun trip to a hospital? Yes, when it involves a ride in a space-age pod that sails ⅔ of a mile (and 500 ft. up) from Oregon Health Science University's Center for Health & Healing at South Waterfront to the main OHSU campus up on Marquam Hill (also known as Pill Hill). On nice days, the $57-million tram offers views of Mt. Hood, Mt. St. Helens, and, of course, the river and downtown. ⏱ *30 min. Departs every 6–10 min. Lower terminal & ticket kiosk at 3303 SW Bond Ave. www.gobytram.com. Admission $4.70 round-trip, free for children 6 & under. Mon–Fri 5:30am–9:30pm, Sat (May–Sept only) 9am–5pm, Sun 1–5pm; closed major holidays. Streetcar: OHSU Commons. Bus: 35 or 36.*

6 ★★ **Tilikum Crossing Bridge.** Right next to the aerial tram, catch the newest extension of the Portland Streetcar (A Loop) and take a ride over the Willamette River via the graceful Tilikum Crossing Bridge, which opened in 2015. The distinctive cable-stayed "Bridge of the People" is the first

The Tilikum Crossing Bridge.

in the country designed exclusively for pedestrians, light-rail, streetcar, and bicycles only (no cars allowed). You can also walk across and pick up the streetcar to OMSI on the other side; along the way you'll enjoy some great views west towards downtown. ⓘ *30 minutes. Streetcars depart every 15–20 min. Streetcar: A Loop from OHSU Commons. Fares: $2 adults, $1 seniors/ ages 7–17.*

❼ ★★ Oregon Museum of Science and Industry. From the giant-screen theater, the heavens-above planetarium, and the submarine docked in the Willamette, to the earthquake simulator and the pint-size science playroom for kids, OMSI is 219,000 square feet of interactive learning and educational fun. *See p 18,* ❽.

❽ Beverly Cleary Sculpture Garden. Fans of the famous children's author will find statues of three of her most beloved characters—Henry Huggins, Ramona Quimby, and Henry's dog, Ribsy— in Grant Park, which appears in several of her books. The statues are just south of the playground near Grant High School, which Cleary also wrote about. Across 33rd Street, the grade school she attended as a child now bears her name. (In the public library branch at NE Tillamook and 40th Ave., a large map of the neighborhood marks more local landmarks in her books.) ⓘ *15 min. NE Brazee St. & NE 33rd Ave. Bus: 73.*

⑨ ★★★ Oaks Amusement Park. A fun-filled time warp on the east bank of the Willamette River near Sellwood, Oaks Amusement Park opened in 1905 to accompany the Lewis and Clark Centennial Exposition. The oldest continually operating amusement park in the country, it has two dozen modern rides, including the Scream-n-Eagle and the Looping Thunder Roller Coaster, along with classics like a Ferris wheel, a Tilt-a-Whirl, go-karts, and a miniature train that chugs along the waterfront. Nostalgists appreciate the 1912 carved carousel, midway games, and roller rink with music from a suspended pipe organ to accompany your skating. There's no charge to enter the park and use its picnic grounds, and a path leads down the bluff to a beach on the river's edge. ○ *2 hr. 7805 SE Oaks Park Way.* ☎ *503/ 233-5777. www.oakspark.com. Free admission to grounds; ride tickets $3.75; unlimited ride tickets $16–$20; roller rink $7–$8. June–Aug Tues– Thurs noon–9pm, Fri–Sat noon–10pm, Sun noon–7pm; open weekends, varying hours, the rest of the year (check website); roller rink open year-round. Bus: 70.*

The Beverly Cleary Sculpture Garden.

Offbeat Portland

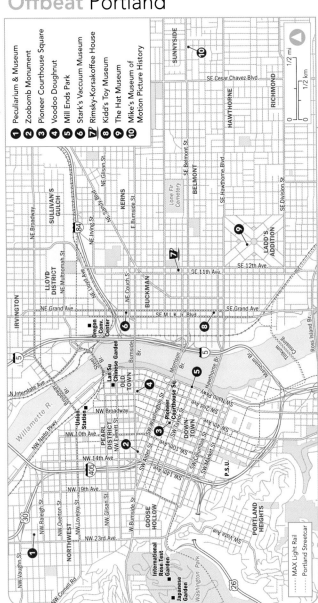

1 Peculiarium & Museum
2 Zoobomb Monument
3 Pioneer Courthouse Square
4 Voodoo Doughnut
5 Mill Ends Park
6 Stark's Vaccuum Museum
7 Rimsky-Korsakoffee House
8 Kidd's Toy Museum
9 The Hat Museum
10 Mike's Museum of Motion Picture History

MAX Light Rail
Portland Streetcar

"**K**eep Portland Weird" isn't just a ubiquitous local bumper sticker; here it's a proud way of life that's still celebrated in the wake of booming gentrification and growing Californication. Whether it's the long cloudy winters or the concentration of creative types (or both), Portland has a streak of strange it wears proudly. And despite all their political correctness, or perhaps because of it, Portlanders still like a good laugh. There's plenty here to amuse your inner oddball, from one-of-a-kind museums to kooky and chaotic annual events. START: **Bus 17 to NW Thurman Ave. & 22nd Pl.**

The wacky Peculiarium & Museum.

❶ ★ Peculiarium & Museum.

Part museum, part art gallery, part gift shop, and part ice-cream parlor, the Peculiarium lives up to its name. In this kingdom of camp, you'll find skulls, vampire-killing kits, and a 10-foot Sasquatch, just for starters. There's an interactive alien autopsy and a motel room painted entirely in glow-in-the-dark paint, plus changing exhibits on things like spontaneous human combustion. Finish off your visit with something from the ice-cream bar, but be warned: The Bug-Eater's Delight is not a descriptive metaphor. Have a look at the website and you'll see what you're in for. ⏱ *30 min. 2234 NW Thurman St.* ☎ *503/227-3164. www.peculiarium.com. $5 for all; dogs in costume get in free. Tues–Thurs 11am–6pm, Fri 11am–8pm, Sun 11am–7pm. Bus: 17.*

❷ ★ Zoobomb monument.

One of the proudest and definitely most unusual traditions in this bike-mad city is the weekly Sunday evening ride—and I use the term loosely—from the zoo down the West Hills. It's the strangest peloton you've ever seen, full of tall bikes, kids' bikes (ridden by adults), skateboards, and essentially

Weird but true: the Zoobomb monument.

anything wheeled and human-powered. Some riders dress in outlandish costumes, and everyone has a blast. If you don't have your own bike, don't worry: Outside the American Apparel store at 13th Avenue and West Burnside Street is a monument (read: pile on a pole) of bikes, including some spares, chained up and waiting for Sunday night. A gold-plated minibike tops the public artwork, also known as the "People's Bike Library of Portland." Zoobomb riders meet here every Sunday around 8:30pm. Bring a bike if you have one, as well as a helmet, MAX fare, and lights. ⏱ *15 min. 13th St. & W. Burnside Ave. www.zoobombpdx.org. Bus: 20.*

❸ kids ★★★ Pioneer Courthouse Square. The most trafficked block in the city still has a few tricks up its sleeves. Throughout the plaza are bricks engraved with the names of donors who helped fund the space—or pseudonyms. See if you can find Mr. Spock, Sherlock Holmes, Jesus Christ, and Bilbo Baggins. (You can order your own

for $100.) The small amphitheater in the northwest corner, below the bronze chess boards, is an echo chamber; if you stand on the central marble stone and speak, it creates a huge echo that only you can hear. Next to the amphitheater is a pole-mounted weather machine. A series of lights show the temperature, and every day at noon, a fanfare announces the weather prediction, indicated by an icon that pops out of the globe on top: a heron for light rain, a dragon for heavy rain, and a sun for, well, sun. On the 6th Avenue side of the plaza, a milepost indicates the distance to places like Mt. Hood, Moscow, Timbuktu, and Tipperary ("a long way"). *See p 9,* **❶**.

❹ kids ★ Voodoo Doughnut. If one place embodies Portland's culture of comestible commercial eccentricity, it's this Old Town eatery where the art of deep-fried pastry circles is taken to new extremes. Doughnuts crusted with Cap'n Crunch and Fruit Loops sit next to Bacon Maple Bars (topped with real

Shanghai Tunnels

In the late 19th century, when Portland was the second-largest port on the West Coast, miles of underground tunnels were built to move goods from the riverside docks into the city. Unfortunately, they were also used to kidnap thousands of drunks and transients from bars, brothels, and boardinghouses to press into service on large sailing ships. Hired thugs used opium knockout drops and trapdoors to grab their prey, receiving payment for each warm body they delivered. At its peak, Portland was said to lead the world in the practice, called *Shanghaiing* because victims often woke up at sea on ships headed to Asia. The tunnels were sealed in 1941, but you can tour them today with **Portland Walking Tours** (☎ 503/774-4522; www.portlandwalkingtours.com). Tours meet outside The Society Hotel (formerly the Old Merchant Hotel) at 131 NW 2nd Ave. (at Davis St.) at 11am and 2pm daily April to November, and Friday and Saturday December to March. The tour lasts about 2 hours and costs $23 adults, $19 seniors and youth 11 to 17, and $9 children 5 to 10.

The gigantic Texas Challenge doughnut at Voodoo Doughnut.

bacon) and the person-shaped Voodoo Doll, filled with raspberry jelly and impaled on a pretzel. If you can eat the giant Texas Challenge in under 80 seconds, it's free. Open 24 hours, Voodoo is popular with late-night revelers, and you can sometimes catch live music or a real live wedding going on, catered with (what else?) coffee and doughnuts. When Voodoo opened its second location at 1501 NE Davis St., there was a bridge-crossing ceremony to transport the hallowed deep-frying oil across the Willamette. ⏱ *30 min. 22 SW 3rd Ave.* ☎ *503/241-4704. www.voodoodoughnut.com. Daily 24 hr. MAX: Skidmore Fountain. Bus: 12, 19, or 20.*

⑤ ★ Mill Ends Park. Portland isn't just home to one of the largest urban parks (Forest Park) in the country; it also boasts the world's smallest, a patch of flowers 24 inches across in the median of SW Naito Parkway at Taylor Street. It started in 1948 when a newspaper journalist, whose office overlooked the road, planted flowers and began writing whimsical columns about a leprechaun named Patrick O'Toole who lived there with his family. It was formally recognized as a city park in 1976—on St. Patrick's Day, of course. ⏱ *5 min. MAX: Yamhill District. Bus: 15 or 51.*

⑥ ★ Stark's Vacuum Museum. Did you know they made vacuums out of cardboard during the Great Depression? You will, after a visit to this display of dirt-suckers through the ages. Part of Stark's Vacuum Cleaner Sales & Service office, most of the 300 models were donated by locals, and include hand-pumped ones from the 19th century and retro-futuristic models from the space-age '60s. The museum was renovated recently to include essential time-lines of how vacuum cleaners developed. Careful—you might just be inspired to leave with a modern Hoover or Dyson. ⏱ *15 min. 107 NE Grand Ave.* ☎ *800/230-4101. www.starks.com. Free admission. Mon–Fri 8am–7pm, Sat 9am–5pm, Sun 11am–5pm. Bus: 6, 2, 19, or 20.*

The most atmospheric coffeehouse in town, and one of the oldest (it was in existence long before the current caffeine craze), **⑦ Rimsky-Korsakoffee House** fills a former Victorian home with oddball art, moving tables, and decorated bathrooms you have to see to believe. The waiters are fun and sassy and the desserts, especially the sundaes, to die for. Some say the place is actually haunted. *707 SE 12th Ave.* ☎ *503/232-2640. $.*

⑧ ★ Kidd's Toy Museum. Fans of antique playthings will love this private collection of hundreds, if not thousands, of toys, games, banks, and other trinkets dating as far back as the 1850s. Frank Kidd has filled one section of his auto parts warehouse with row upon row of vintage trains, soldiers, cars, and trucks. His mechanical cast-iron banks are worth a museum in themselves, with models that show a dentist extracting a tooth or kids peeking at a bathing beauty. (Parent alert: Some items are quite un-PC by modern standards.) Nothing is labeled, not even the building—look for a paper sign taped to the door—but Frank, who's often on site, can give you details on just about anything in his singular collection, which includes dolls and teddy bears his wife has collected. ① 1 hr. 1301 SE Grand Ave. ☎ 503/233-7807. Free admission. Official hours Mon–Thurs noon–6pm, Fri 1–6pm, weekends by appt. Bus: 6.

⑨ ★★ The Hat Museum. One of the country's largest collections of headgear fills a 1910 home in Ladd's Addition, once the home of a talented hatmaker. Over 1,300 hats for men and women, from antique Stetsons to modern tea hats, make up five distinct collections that span the globe. The tour (required) by owner Alyce Cornyn-Selby includes a wealth of detail on the history of hats and their creation. You'll see hats made of cork, mushrooms, feathers, leather, and horsehair. Don't miss the novelty models, like the Thanksgiving table hat that sings and others that fold or hide things inside. The house itself is a curiosity, with secret spaces, mermaid ceiling paintings, and a couch made from a 1966 Cadillac. ① 1½ hr. 1928 SE Ladd Ave. ☎ 503/232-0433. www.thehat museum.com. Tours required by prior appt. only. Deluxe tour $75 for groups of 1–4; individuals $30 1st person, $10 add'l person. Bus: 10.

⑩ ★ Mike's Museum of Motion Picture History. Film buffs know that Movie Madness is the best place in town to find videos and DVDs of classic, independent, and cult movies. It's also home to a collection of costumes and props from films like *The Untouchables* and *Mars Attacks*. Look for Julie Andrews' dress from *The Sound of*

Top things off at the Hat Museum.

Odd Events

At certain times of the year, Portland's peculiarity spikes with annual events that celebrate the eccentric in each of us. On the first Saturday in March, the **Urban Iditarod** replaces huskies with people, sleds with shopping carts, and 1,000 miles through Alaska's thawing permafrost with a 4-mile route across downtown Portland. (The event was canceled as recently as 2015, supposedly because the year before things got out of hand, but never say die; it might occur again.) Outlandish costumes are the rule and everyone's a winner. In mid-June, the 2-week annual bike festival known as Pedalpalooza includes Portland's contribution to the **World Naked Bike Ride,** consisting of thousands—that's right, *thousands*—of unclothed riders taking a bare-assed (and often chilly) spin around town. Held on the third Saturday in August **PDX Adult Soapbox Derby** (www.soapboxracer.com) updates the classic gravity cars of childhood with PhD-level engineering, museum-quality art, and lots of beer. More than 5,000 people gather on the slopes of Mt. Tabor to watch cars hit speeds of over 50 mph, competing for prizes in decoration, velocity, and crowd-pleasing.

If you happen to see a large group of boisterous Santas careening around town in early December, chances are it's the latest incarnation of **SantaCon** (www.pdxcacophony.org), a mix of holiday spirit, performance art, and inebriated rowdiness organized by the Portland Cacophony Society (motto: "Life is short. Mess with someone else's.").

The Adult Soapbox Derby.

Music and Orson Welles's jacket from *Touch of Evil,* a classic 1958 film noir. ⏱ *45 min. 4320 SE Belmont St.* ☎ *503/234-4363.*

www.moviemadnessvideo.com/ museum. Free admission. Daily 11am–11pm. Bus: 15.

Rainy Day Portland

1 Portland Japanese Garden
2 Portland Art Museum
3 Central Library
4 Powell's City of Books
5 Ground Kontrol Classic Arcade
6 Floyd's Coffee Shop Old Town
7 Lan Su Chinese Garden
8 Portland Rock Gym
9 Bagdad Theater & Pub
10 Oaks Skating Rink

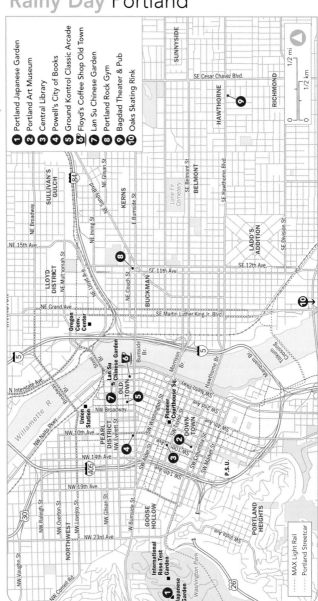

MAX Light Rail
Portland Streetcar

1/2 mi
1/2 km

It's a fact of life: from fall through spring, and especially in the winter, Portland gets a lot of rain. But that doesn't mean there still isn't plenty to do when the clouds roll in and the misty Northwest drizzle begins. Most of the activities on this tour are indoors, for obvious reasons, but a few outdoor ones take advantage of the moody change in atmosphere overcast skies can bring. So get out your rubber boots and rain jackets—Portlanders are notoriously averse to umbrellas—and head out into the drops. START: **MAX to Washington Park. Bus 63 on weekdays.**

❶ ★★★ Portland Japanese Garden. Washington Park's world-class Japanese garden is just as enchanting in the rain as it is in the sun. Like most classical Japanese gardens, it's designed with the changing seasons in mind, with certain scenes best viewed in the rain (or snow, for that matter). The rough stones, meticulously trimmed shrubs, surrounding forest, glowing mosses, and placid koi pond take on a different, softer, yet still serene look in the moist atmosphere. And you can always duck into Kengo Kuma's gorgeous pavilion with its gift shop and gallery, or the glass-walled teahouse that floats above the hillside. *See p 15,* **❶**.

❷ ★★ Portland Art Museum. Spend an hour indoors drying off

with Marcel Duchamp, Gustave Courbet, Albert Bierstadt, and Ansel Adams—or at least their works—at Portland's best-known art institution. Time it right to catch a free gallery tour, lecture, or Mid-day Art Break. *Tours Sun–Fri 12:30pm and occasionally in the afternoon. See p 10,* **❸**.

❸ ★ kids Central Library. The main branch of the Multnomah County Library, opened in 1913, fills a massive Georgian-style building downtown with 875 *tons* of books on some 17 miles of bookshelves. Just stepping inside is inspiring, with the sweeping main staircase climbing through a three-story atrium. The **Beverly Cleary Children's Library,** named after the famous local author, has a sculpture

An eye-opening installation at the Portland Art Museum.

of Alice in Wonderland and a 14-foot bronze tree covered in carved images from kids' books like *The Wizard of Oz* and *The Little Engine That Could*. On the third floor, the **Collins Gallery** hosts rotating art exhibits, and the **John Wilson Special Collections** focus on Pacific Northwest history, children's literature, and Native American books. ⏱ *30 min. 801 SW 10th Ave.* ☎ *503/988-5123. www.multcolib.org. Mon, Thurs & Sat 10am–6pm, Tues–Wed 10am–8pm, Sun noon–5pm. Streetcar: Central Library. MAX: Library/SW 9th Ave.*

④ ★★★ kids Powell's City of Books. Satisfy any lingering literary cravings at Portland's world-class independent bookseller. Browse through 3,500 sections, including an outstanding **children's section** in the first-floor Rose Room. The **Basil Hallward Gallery,** upstairs in the Pearl Room, hosts new art exhibits every month, and the **World Cup coffee shop** has plenty of seats for browsing and watching the rain fall through its big windows. *See p 10,* ④.

⑤ ★ kids Ground Kontrol Classic Arcade. If you spent a good chunk of your childhood weekends in video arcades, this two-story retro game room will whisk you back to the days of honing your skills at Centipede and Donkey Kong. Ground Kontrol has more than 90 cabinet games from the past 40 years, from oldies like Asteroids and Tempest to the newest, like the four-player Pac-Man Battle Royale. And they're all still only a quarter! Get a workout on Dance Dance Revolution in the back corner, or head upstairs for dozens of pinball machines. A full bar serves drinks and snacks, and DJs spin music in the evenings. Every second Thursday and last Wednesday evening of the month, admission is free. ⏱ *45 min. 511 NW Couch St.* ☎ *503/796-9364. www.groundkontrol.com. Free admission. Daily noon–late; ages 21 & over only after 5pm. MAX: NW 5th & Couch St.*

Retro games and pinball machines at Ground Kontrol Classic Arcade.

A tea tasting at the Lan Su Chinese Garden.

Serving Stumptown coffee in the ambiance of an old diner, **6 Floyd's Coffee Shop Old Town** (there's another one on the East Side) has comfy seating, inexpensive eats, and outstanding espresso drinks, perfect for a respite from the drizzle. *118 NW Couch St.* ☎ *503/295-7791. MAX: Old Town/Chinatown. Bus: 12, 19, 20. $.*

7 ★★★ Lan Su Chinese Garden. Like the Portland Japanese Garden (p 15), this remarkable walled garden in the heart of Chinatown was designed to be appreciated in any kind of weather. Covered walkways lead between ornate pavilions with names like "Painted Boat in Misty Rain" and "Flowers Bathing in Spring Rain." Banana plants are positioned under rain gutters to create a distinctive sound when splashed with water. The Chinese Garden is a peaceful place to spend a damp afternoon, particularly the teahouse, where you can linger over a pot of lapsang souchong and contemplate Lake Zither. *See p 17,* **5**.

8 ★★ Portland Rock Gym. Rock climbing in the rain? Sure, when it's inside the state's largest rock gym. Walls 35 feet high are studded with artificial climbing holds, offering an ever-changing selection of 100 climbing routes at all levels, each flagged with colored tape. In case you've never climbed before, they offer instruction and gear rental, as well as a weight room, cardio machines, and yoga and Pilates classes. Ropes are mandatory in the main room, but in the bouldering area you can learn this low-level skill (you're never more than a few feet off the padded floor) without being "tied in." Expert climbers can tackle the 16-foot overhang or dozens of lead-climbing routes. ⏱ *1 hr. 21 NE 12th Ave.* ☎ *503/232-8310. www.portlandrockgym.com. Mon, Wed & Fri 11am–11pm, Tues & Thurs 7am–11pm, Sat 9am–9pm, Sun 9am–6pm. Day pass $19 adults ($13 before 3pm Mon–Fri), $13 children 11 & under, $9.50 seniors 62 & older on weekdays. Bus: 12, 19, 20, or 70.*

The restored Bagdad Theater & Pub.

9 ★★ Bagdad Theater & Pub.

Sometimes all you want to do on an overcast evening is eat pizza, drink beer, and watch a movie. This proud artifact of the Golden Age of Hollywood lets you do all of that with a little style. Built by Universal Pictures in 1927, the Bagdad survived the transition from vaudeville to "talkies" and hosted everyone from Sammy Davis, Jr., to Jack Nicholson and Michael Douglas, here for the 1975 premiere of *One Flew Over the Cuckoo's Nest* (based on Oregon author Ken Kesey's novel about an Oregon lumber family). Since taking over the property in the early 1990s, the McMenamin brothers have restored the movie palace to all its faux–Middle Eastern glory, including wrought-iron fixtures, tiled arches, and paintings. The pub serves pizza, burgers, and handcrafted ales, all of which you can bring into the theater for movies and the occasional comedy show or author reading. (Don't miss the Backstage Bar behind the screen, with its seven-story ceiling.) ⏰ *1–2 hr. 3702 SE Hawthorne Blvd.* ☎ *503/467-7521. www.mcmenamins.com/bagdad. Tickets $2–$28. Pub Mon–Thurs 11am–midnight, Fri–Sat 11am–1am, Sun noon–midnight. Backstage Bar Mon–Thurs 5pm–midnight, Fri 5pm–2:30am, Sat 2pm–2:30am, Sun 2pm–midnight. Bus: 14.*

10 ★★ kids Oaks Amusement Park Skating Rink.

The weather is an afterthought inside the vintage skating rink at Oaks Amusement Park, open (like the park itself) since 1905. It's a roll through the halls of nostalgia, circling the lovingly maintained wooden floor beneath the working Wurlitzer pipe organ. You can rent skates, grab a snack, and even take a lesson on weekends. *See p 31,* 9. ●

Downtown Portland

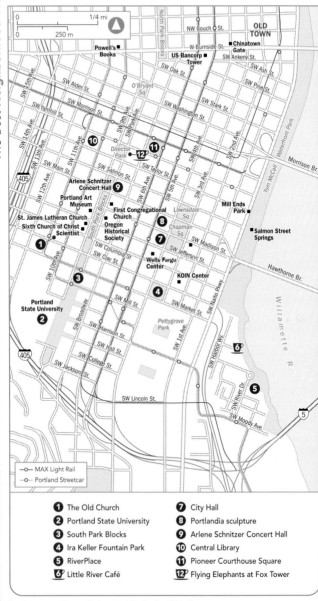

0 ——— 1/4 mi
0 ——— 250 m

Powell's Books

O'Bryant Sq

US Bancorp Tower

Chinatown Gate

OLD TOWN

Director Park

Arlene Schnitzer Concert Hall ❾

Portland Art Museum ■

St. James Lutheran Church

Sixth Church of Christ, Scientist

First Congregational Church ■

Oregon Historical Society

Mill Ends Park ■

Salmon Street Springs

Wells Fargo Center

KOIN Center

Portland State University ❷

Pettygrove Park

Willamette R.

-o— MAX Light Rail
-o— Portland Streetcar

❶ The Old Church
❷ Portland State University
❸ South Park Blocks
❹ Ira Keller Fountain Park
❺ RiverPlace
❻ Little River Café

❼ City Hall
❽ Portlandia sculpture
❾ Arlene Schnitzer Concert Hall
❿ Central Library
⓫ Pioneer Courthouse Square
⓬ Flying Elephants at Fox Tower

Previous page: Tanner Springs Park in the Pearl District.

Downtown Portland is surprisingly compact and manageable. Busy as it may be, it's still possible to walk from one end of the central downtown core to the other in 30 minutes or less. Along with office and government buildings, downtown is home to Oregon's largest university (Portland State) as well as plenty of shops, cafes, restaurants, and cultural venues. Alternatives to walking or biking are the MAX light rail, buses, or the streetcar. START: Streetcar at SW 11th & Clay, bus: 6, 43, 45, 55, 58, or 68.

① ★★ The Old Church. Built of wood in an ornate style known as Carpenter Gothic, this Victorian beauty started as a Presbyterian church in 1883, making it one of the oldest buildings in the Pacific Northwest. Today it's owned by a nonprofit organization and hosts concerts, lectures, and other public events. Many of the original architectural features have been preserved, including hand-carved fir pews and built-in umbrella racks. ① *15 min. 1422 SW 11th Ave.* ☎ *503/222-2031. www.oldchurch.org. Mon–Fri 11am– 3pm. Self-guided tours are free; admission varies by scheduled event.*

② ★ Portland State University. With 30,000 students, the largest university in Oregon anchors the southern end of downtown with its leafy 49-acre urban campus. Several significant public spaces added by recent building on campus co-mingle student activities and the downtown community. Streetcar lines pass through the campus center. **Lincoln Hall** (1620 SW Park Ave.)

serves as a concert hall and performing arts space. ① *15 min. Btw. SW Market St., SW 3rd Ave. & I-405.* ☎ *503/725-3000. www.pdx.edu.*

③ ★★ South Park Blocks. Thank Portland cofounder Daniel Lownsdale for this strip of 12 grassy blocks leading from the PSU campus into the center of downtown. Four years after buying up most of what would become downtown Portland in 1848, Lownsdale donated the land to the city (some say, to guard his property from forest fires). The southernmost of the Park Blocks are home to the Portland Farmers Market on Saturdays from March to December (p 80). Significant buildings in this area include the **Portland Art Museum** designed by Pietro Belluschi in 1932 (see p. 10, **③**); the **Oregon Historical Society** (see p. 16, **④**); the 1920s-era **Arlene Schnitzer Concert Hall** (see below, **⑨**); the 1931 brick Byzantine-style **Sixth Church of Christ Scientist** (corner of SW Park and SW Columbia); the Venetian Gothic **First**

The Ira Keller Fountain evokes Northwest mountain waterfalls.

Benson Bubblers

In 1912, a local lumber baron, philanthropist, and teetotaler named Simon Benson noticed that his mill workers' breath smelled of booze. Upon learning that fresh water was hard to find downtown, Benson donated $10,000 to the city to install 20 bronze drinking fountains. (His ploy worked: Beer consumption allegedly fell 25%.) There are now 52 "Benson bubblers" throughout Portland, mostly downtown, including the original four-bowl fountain at SW 5th Avenue and Washington Street. (Another 74 single-bowl versions were added later.) They're cleaned regularly and flow daily with fresh drinking water from the Bull Run watershed.

One of the many Benson Bubbler drinking fountains around downtown

Congregational United Church of Christ from 1895 (corner of SW Park and SW Madison); and the 1891 Late Gothic Revival **St. James' Lutheran** (corner of SW Park and SW Jefferson). 🕐 *30 min. SW Park Ave. btw. Salmon & Hall sts. Open daily.*

❹ ★★ kids Ira Keller Fountain Park. When this urban park and waterfall designed by San Francisco landscape architect Lawrence Halprin was unveiled in 1970, *New York Times* architectural critic Ada Louise Huxtable hailed it "the greatest public fountain since the Renaissance." Maybe that's overdoing it, but the fountain's impressive design with pools, streams, stepping stones, and tall vertical planes (all made of concrete) is meant to evoke Oregon's many mountain waterfalls. You can walk to the top and look over (there's a 3-foot lip hidden under the water at the edge). 🕐 *15 min. SW 3rd Ave. & SW Clay St.*

❺ ★★ RiverPlace. Portland's urban downtown meets its lifeblood river here at this modern 50-acre development between the noisy Marquam (I-5) and Hawthorne bridges. RiverPlace combines condos, townhomes, shops, and a hotel with a public marina and a popular riverbank park; an extension of the riverfront pedestrian esplanade leads past a row of shops and restaurants that are busy on sunny afternoons. The octagonal Newport Seafood Grill anchors the floating breakwater. 🕐 *30 min. Btw. SW Harbor Way & SW Montgomery St. Streetcar: SW River Pkwy. & Moody.*

Tasty soups and sandwiches are available at the snug **❻ Little River Café** in the middle of the RiverPlace esplanade. There's not much space inside, but the outside seats are great for people- and river-watching. *0315 SW Montgomery St. #310.* ☎ *503/227-2327. www. littlerivercafe.com. Hours vary with season; summer daily 7am–8:30pm. $.*

7 ★ City Hall. Built in 1895, the home of Portland's City Council underwent a full renovation in the 1990s, restoring the four-story Italianate building to its original glory. Commissioned artworks, both permanent and temporary, decorate the interior. ⏱ 15 min. 1221 SW 4th Ave. ☎ 503/823-4000. www.portland online.com. Mon–Fri 9am–4pm.

8 ★★ Portlandia sculpture. Before *Portlandia* the TV series, there was *Portlandia* the sculpture: the nation's second-largest hammered-copper statue, after the Statue of Liberty. Based on the city seal, the 34-foot-high "Lady Commerce," installed in 1985, kneels over the entrance to Michael Graves' ugly and much-despised postmodern Portland Building, holding a trident in one hand and reaching down with the other. ⏱ 5 min. 1120 SW 5th Ave. btw. Madison & Main sts.

9 ★ Arlene Schnitzer Concert Hall. The most historic of Portland's Centers for the Arts, "the Schnitz," as it's known locally, is the last of the grand old theaters that once lined Broadway. Built in 1928, it was a vaudeville house and movie theater before being restored in 1984 to its original Hollywood Moorish splendor. The distinctive 65-foot "Portland" sign outside is lit with more than 5,000 lights; inside, look for a statue of a scantily clad woman with her hands over her face (titled *Surprise*), missing two fingers that were shot off in a gunfight during a movie in the 1950s. The Schnitz is the home of the superlative Oregon Symphony and a venue for big-name performers and events. 1037 SW Broadway at Main St. ⏱ 5 min. ☎ 503/248-4335. www.pcpa. com. Ticket prices & showtimes vary.

10 ★ kids Central Library. There's something for everyone at the Multnomah County Library's main branch, a Georgian-style building with a grand central staircase, three-story atrium, and cozy children's library. See p 39, **3**.

11 ★★★ kids Pioneer Courthouse Square. Shoemaker Elijah Hill purchased this downtown block in 1849 for $24 and a pair of high boots. It later became the site of the city's first school and after that, the grand Portland Hotel, which was knocked down to make the parking lot that was here before the square was completely redone in the 1970s for people instead of cars. The 1875 Pioneer Courthouse, stands at the square's east end. See p 9, **1**.

For a good and casual nosh, visit **12 Flying Elephants at Fox Tower,** an all-purpose deli right on Teacher's Park, where you'll find soups, sandwiches, salads, and sweets. 812 SW Park Ave. ☎ 503/546-3166. $.

Pioneer Courthouse Square is a prime spot for people-watching.

The Pearl District & Old Town

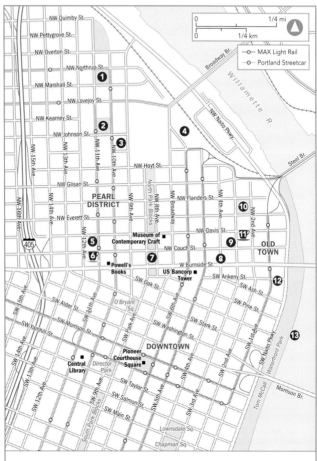

1 Tanner Springs Park
2 Jamison Square Park
3 Ecotrust Building
4 Union Station
5 The Armory
6 Peet's Coffee & Tea
7 North Park Blocks
8 Chinatown Gateway

9 Hung Far Low sign
10 Lan Su Chinese Garden
11 Old Town Pizza
12 Ankeny Plaza
13 Oregon Maritime Museum

A few blocks northwest of downtown, Portland neighborhoods run the gamut from the upscale Pearl District to the slightly more disheveled streets of Old Town and Chinatown. Once a blue-collar district of warehouses and light industry, "the Pearl" is a case study in urban revitalization at its best, while Old Town holds on to its history, at least architecturally. (By the way, "Couch" street is pronounced "cooch," not like the piece of furniture.) START: Streetcar NW 10th and Marshall.

❶ ★★ **Tanner Springs Park.** A quiet haven of burbling water and reedy grasses, this park re-creates a pocket of Portland's original wetlands and the stream that ran through it. A short walking trail leads past benches along a creek, and the east edge has a striking art installation: a wavelike wall of rusted railroad tracks studded with blue glass. ⏱ *15 min. NW Marshall & 11th aves.*

❷ ★★ 🄺🄸🄳🄢 **Jamison Square Park.** Just 2 blocks away is another water-centric park, this one focused on a large fountain designed to mimic a tidal pool, with water spilling over low steps into a shallow pool that periodically empties and refills. Take a look at the contemporary totem poles on 10th Street,

the red-granite statue of a brown bear, and the urbane little French-style bosque. The park is named for William Jamison, whose art gallery got the Pearl District revitalization going in the 1990s. ⏱ *15 min. NW Johnson & 10th aves.*

❸ ★ **Ecotrust Building.** One of the greenest of Portland's green buildings, this 2001 building made of recycled materials is now home to a collection of sustainable businesses. Portions of the original 1895 warehouse still stand along NW 10th Avenue. ⏱ *5 min. 721 NW 9th Ave.*

❹ ★★ **Union Station.** Portland's grand rail terminal, built in 1896, reflected the city's position at the western end of the only sea-level route through the Cascade

The water-centric Jamison Square Park.

Mountains. The Italian Renaissance–style building was renovated in 1996 after a century of use. Luckily, it kept its signature 150-foot Romanesque clock tower with its landmark "Go By Train" sign. You can get a taste of the building's glory days inside at Amtrak's only first-class Metropolitan Lounge on the West Coast, as well as at **Wilfs,** 800 NW 6th Ave. (☎ 503/223-0070; www.wilfsrestaurant.com), which combines turn-of-the-century ambience with organic local produce and live jazz from Wednesday through Saturday night. ⏱ *15 min. 800 NW 6th Ave. at Irving St.* ☎ *503/273-4865.*

⑤ The Armory. Yet another historic building saved from the wrecking ball and repurposed, this unmistakable brick fortress anchors the downtown "Brewery Blocks." Constructed in 1891 to house the Oregon National Guard, it hosted presidential speeches, symphony concerts, and many, many casks of beer over the next century. A 2006 renovation made it one of the greenest buildings in the country—we're talking LEED platinum status—and the new home of **Portland Center Stage,** the city's largest theater company, with the 600-seat Gerding Theater, a small studio theater, and a cafe. Step into the lobby to see the grand staircase cantilevered off the second-floor balcony and the enormous ceiling trusses that give it such a roomy feel. ⏱ *15 min. 128 NW 11th Ave. at Davis St.* ☎ *503/445-3700. www.pcs.org. Ticket prices & showtimes vary.*

Recharge at **⑥ Peet's Coffee & Tea,** a long-established West Coast brand that serves strong coffee, chai lattes, tea drinks, and pastries. *1114 NW Couch.* ☎ *971/244-0452. $.*

⑦ ★ kids North Park Blocks. Disconnected from the South Park Blocks by West Burnside Street, the North Park Blocks have a more urban feel than their counterparts, even though they have just as many old trees lining their sidewalks. The playground and basketball court are both popular, as are various artworks. Look for the 12-foot bronze elephant sculpture between Burnside and Couch streets, an oversize replica of a Shang Dynasty wine pitcher, given to the city by a Chinese foundry owner. William Wegman, known for his photos of Weimaraner dogs, designed the checkerboard granite tiles of the "Portland Dog Bowl" between Davis and Everett streets to mimic a linoleum kitchen floor. Think of the bronze water bowl as a canine version of the Benson bubbler fountains (p 46). ⏱ *15 min. NW Park Ave. from Ankeny St. to Glisan St. Open daily.*

⑧ ★ Chinatown Gateway. This ornate arch, built in 1985, is an

Lion statues guard the Chinatown Gateway.

impressive monument to the long history of Portland's Chinese residents. Artisans from Taiwan put it together and installed the two lion statues on either side. (The one on the left, Yin, protects the young, and Yang, the one on the right, protects the country.) The 38-foot high structure is decorated with 78 dragons and 58 mythical characters, including the Chinese characters for "Portland Chinatown" on the south side and "Four Seas, One Family" on the north side. ⏱ *5 min. NW 4th Ave. at Burnside St.*

❾ ★ Hung Far Low sign. Chinatown's other landmark earns its share of giggles, but this pagoda-topped marquee advertised a real restaurant here from 1928 to 2005. (Like many Chinese-owned businesses in Portland, it relocated to SE 82nd Ave.) The two-story, 2,000-pound neon sign was restored and–ahem–re-erected in 2010. ⏱ *5 min. NW 4th Ave. at Couch St.*

❿ ★★★ Lan Su Chinese Garden. Complete your Chinatown visit with a stop at this astonishingly authentic classical Chinese garden, occupying a full block on the neighborhood's eastern side. You'll feel like you've stepped off a boat in ancient Suzhou, the coastal Chinese city where the entire garden was designed, packed up, and exported to be reassembled here in 2001. A teahouse in the lakeside **Tower of Cosmic Reflections** (☎ 503/224-8455) offers a contemplative spot to watch the light change over the plantings, Lake Zither, and the array of classical Chinese pavilions and walkways. *See p 17, ❺.*

At the distinctive **⓫ Old Town Pizza,** a pizzeria housed in a former hotel, step up to the old reception desk to order a slice, and keep an eye out for Nina, the resident ghost. *226 NW Davis St.* ☎ *503/222-9999. $.*

The serene Lan Su Chinese Garden.

White Stag Sign

One of Portland's most distinctive icons greets drivers and cyclists crossing the Burnside Bridge into downtown: a bounding neon stag above the words "Portland Oregon," enclosed by an outline of the state. The wording has gone through more revisions than a breakup letter, starting in 1940 when it was built to advertise White Satin Sugar. The building's next tenant conveniently shared an adjective, so the sign read "White Stag Sportswear" until 1995, when it was changed to read "Made in Oregon," with "Old Town" the latest subtitle. The current arrangement went up in 2010. (If you're around during the holidays, notice how easily the stag is transformed into Rudolph the Red-Nosed Reindeer.)

The iconic White Stag sign.

⑫ ★ **Ankeny Plaza.** Once the city's nexus of business and entertainment, this triangular plaza in Old Town is now home to the popular **Portland Saturday Market** of craft vendors (see p 78). At the plaza's center, you'll see the neoclassical bronze and granite **Skidmore Fountain,** the oldest piece of public art in the city. For the fountain's grand opening in 1888, local brewer Henry Weinhard offered to pump beer through it using firehoses. (For some reason,

The Skidmore Fountain at Ankeny Plaza.

city leaders turned him down.) Many of the nearby buildings, built of brick and cast iron in the late 19th century, are part of the Skidmore/Old Town National Historic District. ⏱ *15 min. SW 1st Ave. & SW Ankeny St.*

⓭ ★ **kids Oregon Maritime Museum.** After the steam-powered sternwheeler tug *Portland*—the last of its kind to operate in the United States—was retired in 1981 after 3 decades of service, it was restored to house a collection of maritime artifacts, ship models, and other nautical memorabilia. Youngsters can putter around a children's corner with a working ship's whistle and other hands-on attractions. The ship itself is the real attraction, though, as you'll discover on a tour with one of the expert docents, who will lead you around from pilot house to engine room. ⏱ *45 min. On the Willamette River in Waterfront Park, at Pine St.* ☎ *503/224-7724. www.oregonmaritimemuseum. org. Wed & Fri–Sat 11am–4pm. Admission $7 adults, $5 seniors, $3 children 6–17.*

Northwest Portland

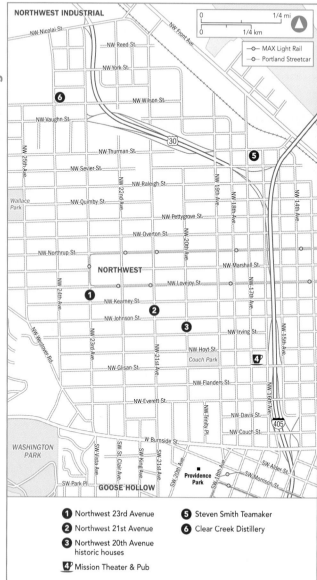

NORTHWEST INDUSTRIAL

NW Nicolai St.
NW Reed St.
NW York St.
NW Front Ave.
NW Wilson St.
NW Vaughn St.
NW Thurman St.
NW Sevier St.
NW Raleigh St.
NW Quimby St.
NW Pettygrove St.
NW Overton St.
NW Northrup St.
NORTHWEST
NW Marshall St.
NW Lovejoy St.
NW Kearney St.
NW Johnson St.
NW Irving St.
NW Hoyt St.
Couch Park
NW Glisan St.
NW Flanders St.
NW Everett St.
NW Davis St.
NW Trinity Pl.
NW Couch St.
W Burnside St.

WASHINGTON PARK
SW Alder St.
SW Morrison St.
Providence Park
GOOSE HOLLOW
SW Park Pl.

Wallace Park

NW 25th Ave.
NW 22nd Ave.
NW 19th Ave.
NW 18th Ave.
NW 14th Ave.
NW 20th Ave.
NW 17th Ave.
NW 15th Ave.
NW 16th Ave.
NW 24th Ave.
NW 23rd Ave.
NW 21st Ave.
NW Westover Rd.
SW Vista Ave.
SW St. Clair Ave.
SW King Ave.
SW 21st Ave.
SW 18th Ave.

30
405

| 0 | | 1/4 mi |
| 0 | | 1/4 km |

—o— MAX Light Rail
—o— Portland Streetcar

1 Northwest 23rd Avenue
2 Northwest 21st Avenue
3 Northwest 20th Avenue historic houses
4 Mission Theater & Pub
5 Steven Smith Teamaker
6 Clear Creek Distillery

Portland's northwest corner is a neighborhood of tree-shaded Victorian homes, postwar apartment buildings, and old and new mansions overlooking downtown and the river. It's one of the city's wealthier districts, with Arlington Heights and Forest Park rising to the west of Nob Hill, which is the oldest part of northwest Portland and not really much of a hill at all. On weekends and during the summer, visitors flock to the destination shopping and dining streets, NW 21st and NW 23rd avenues. START: **Bus: 15 or 77; Streetcar: NW 23rd & Marshall.**

❶ ★★★ Northwest 23rd Avenue.

From West Burnside to Thurman Street, NW 23rd Avenue is an almost continuous string of restaurants, cafes, boutiques, coffee shops, and bars. Detractors may dismiss it as "trendy-third," but it's the commercial heart of Northwest Portland, and definitely one of the destination shopping and dining stretches in Portland. There's a lovely residential area around NW 23rd and Lovejoy, where most of the Victorian- and Edwardian-era homes are located, called **Nob Hill** because it was built to rival San Francisco's neighborhood of the same name. The south end near Burnside is home to large chain stores like Pottery Barn, Urban Outfitters, and Restoration. As you head north, you'll find more smaller and more distinctive local shops. Businesses peter out around Thurman Street, but take a left (west) for another 6 long blocks of options, plus, eventually, one of the main entrances to **Forest Park** (see p 86). 🕐 *1½ hr.*

❷ ★ Northwest 21st Avenue.

Two blocks east, NW 21st Avenue leans more toward the food and

Cafe latte at Ken's Artisan Bakery on NW 21st Avenue.

A Swift September

Every evening in September, about an hour before sunset, hundreds of people congregate around Chapin Elementary School, which sits in the middle of Wallace Park (west of NW 25th Ave. btw. Pettygrove and Raleigh sts.). They bring their own chairs or blankets and camp out to watch a very special phenomenon: the Swift Watch. Thousands of migrating Vaux's swifts circle in a vortexlike cloud around the school's chimney, before flying in to roost for the night. If you're a birder, or have kids, this is a sight worth planning for. For information, go to **www.audubonportland.org**.

drink side of things rather than shopping. Take your pick from outstanding pastries at **Ken's Artisan Bakery** (338 NW 21st Ave. at Flanders), a chic Italian bar and restaurant at **Caffe Mingo** (807 NW 21st Ave. at Kearney St.), or French-Russian cooking at **Paley's Place** (1204 NW 21st Ave. at Northrup St.). The **Chop Butchery & Charcuterie** (735 NW 21st Ave. at Johnson St.) offers sandwiches and all things meat. The avenue is not all about eating, though; **Cinema 21** (616 NW 21st Ave. at Irving St.) shows independent and art-house movies.
🕐 1½ hr.

❸ ★ **Northwest 20th Avenue historic houses.** Gorgeous homes from the 1890s to the 1930s are everywhere in this Northwest neck of the woods, but you can find three excellent examples within a few blocks of Irving Street on 20th Avenue. (Keep in mind they're all private homes.) The 1892 Richardsonian Romanesque Revival at 615 NW 20th Ave. at Hoyt Street has the slate shingles, substantial stonework, and arched entrance porch that recall other examples of the style (such as Trinity Church in

Boston and the American Museum of Natural History in New York City). The 1908 Colonial Revival at 733 NW 20th Ave. at Johnson Street was designed after a mid-18th-century Georgian colonial home in Pennsylvania, and the 1910 Craftsman at 811 NW 20th Ave. at Johnson Street is another example of the simple but handsome style.
🕐 30 min.

The singular ❹ **Mission Theater & Pub** started as a Swedish Evangelical Mission in 1912, then served as a Longshoreman's Union hall before becoming Oregon's first theater-pub. Sit in the balcony or on the floor for recent movies, cult films, live music, or sporting events projected on a big screen. It's a McMenamins joint, so, of course, pub fare, handcrafted ales, and wine are on sale. Thursday is pizza, pint, and popcorn night for $10. *1624 NW Glisan St. at 17th Ave.* ☎ *503/223-4527. www.mcmenamins. com. Admission $4 adults, $3 children 11 and under. Age 21 and over only, unless accompanied by parent. Event hours vary.*

⑤ ★ Steven Smith Teamaker. The local founder of both Stash Tea and Tazo Tea has launched his own line of small-batch teas using rare, high-quality ingredients. You can come by the facility, an old blacksmith shop, to taste a cup or see the teas being made and packaged. If you're inspired, you can even blend your own batch. ⏱ 30 min. 1626 NW Thurman St. ☎ 503/719-8752 or 800/624-9531. www.smithtea.com. Mon–Fri 9am–5pm. Free admission.

⑥ ★ Clear Creek Distillery. Traditional European brandy-making techniques meet northwest Oregon's bounty of fruit at this artisan distillery, producer of fruit eaux de vie, grappas, and wine brandies. They only offer public tours around Memorial Day and Thanksgiving, but their tasting room and store are open year-round. Come by to learn about the process and sample spirits like their pear eaux de vie, with the pear grown inside the bottle, or their Islay-style Oregon single malt whiskey. ⏱ 30 min. 2389 NW Wilson St. ☎ 503/248-9470. www.clear creekdistillery.com. Mon–Sat 9am–5pm. Free admission.

A spirits tasting at Clear Creek Distillery.

The Best Neighborhood Walks

Northeast Portland: Irvington, Alameda & Alberta Arts District

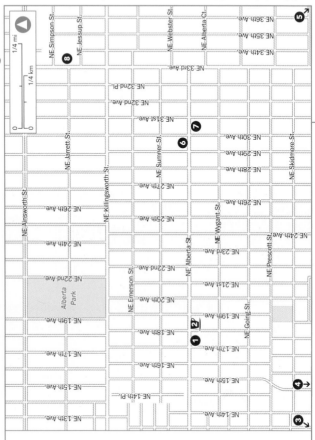

1 Community Cycling Center
2 Random Order Pie Bar
3 Irving Park
4 Backyard Bird Shop
5 Alameda Ridge Neighborhood
6 Guardino Gallery
7 Alberta Rose Theatre
8 McMenamins Kennedy School

Northeast Portland is home to two of the oldest neighborhoods outside of the city center. Irvington is primarily a residential neighborhood, filled with a wonderful array of houses dating from the early 1900s to the late 1940s. Adjoining Irvington to the north, Northeast Alberta Street between 12th and 33rd avenues—now known as the Alberta Arts District—has been "discovered" by young professionals looking for affordable real estate and a diverse cultural mix, where Hispanic, Asian, and African-American businesses rub shoulders with hip cafes, boutiques, and trendy eateries. Alameda is another long-established and attractive residential neighborhood with winding streets along Alameda Ridge, which provides views back towards downtown. START: **Bus 8 or 72.**

❶ ★ Community Cycling Center. Few places embody Portland's two-wheeled ethos as robustly as this nonprofit bike shop. They don't just fix and sell bikes, parts, and accessories—they also offer year-round programs that help get citizens up and rolling, including bike camps, bike clubs, maintenance classes, and bike drives for low-income families. ⏱ *15 min. 1700 NE Alberta St. at 17th Ave.* ☎ *503/287-8786. www.communitycycling center.org. Tues–Sun 10am–6pm.*

Refuel at **❷ Random Order Coffeehouse & Bakery** with a cup of java and a slice of homemade pie, either sweet or savory. Brandied peach and salted caramel apple are both specialties, and the Catalan vegetable potpie is enough for a meal. *1800 NE Alberta St. at 18th Ave.* ☎ *971/340-6995. www.random ordercoffee.com. Mon 6:30am–8pm, Tues–Sun 6:30am–11pm. $.*

The colorful mural of Community Cycling Center.

The Simpsons in Portland?

If some of the street names in Portland sound familiar, thank local son Matt Groening, creator of the TV hits *The Simpsons* and *Futurama,* who grew up in the Rose City. In the Alphabet District, look for (Montgomery) Burns(ide), (Ned) Flanders, (Reverend) Lovejoy, and (Mayor) Quimby Streets. The Springfield Gorge and the Murderhorn, Springfield's highest peak, echo the Columbia River Gorge and Mt. Hood. And the benighted nuclear power plant where Homer Simpson works may have been based on the Trojan Nuclear Power Plant in Rainier, 46 miles north. It was decommissioned after 16 years due to safety and seismic concerns. D'oh!

❸ ★ Irving Park. Portland is loaded with great neighborhood parks like this 16-acre oasis in the heart of Irvington. The park (and the neighborhood) was named for William Irving, a 19th-century mariner. It was created in 1920 on part of Irving's land claim and signaled the rapid growth of the residential Irvington neighborhood. ⏱ *10 min.*

❹ ★ kids Backyard Bird Shop. Birding is big in Portland, so if you have any interest in our winged wonders, head over to this shop. It's not fancy, but it carries just about everything you need to nurture the birds in your backyard. There are feeders of every size, shape, and description, plus bulk birdseed mixes, birdhouses, birdbaths, and more. ⏱ *5 min. 1419 NE Fremont.* ☎ *503/455-2699. www.backyardbirdshop.com. Mon–Sat 10am–6pm, Sun 10am–5pm.*

❺ ★★ Alameda Ridge Neighborhood. Alameda, one of Portland's most charming northeast

neighborhoods, lies along winding Alameda Ridge between NE 23rd Ave. and NE 33rd Ave. with views south and west towards downtown. In the 1920s and 1930s, grand homes and English-style cottages were constructed in this new (and highly restricted) development. ⏱ *15 min.*

❻ ★ Guardino Gallery. Of all the galleries on Alberta Street, Guardino has the most reliably exciting mix of works and styles. From bronze sculptures and acrylic paintings to prints made with rusted car parts on old silk, there's always something unexpectedly intriguing on display. In the same building, you'll find the **HiiH Gallery,** selling handmade paper lamps, and **Redbird Studio,** with handmade cards, antique stationery, clothes, and crafts. ⏱ *1 hr. 2939 NE Alberta St. at 29th Ave.* ☎ *503/281-9048. www.guardino gallery.com. Tues 11am–5pm, Wed–Sat 11am–6pm, Sun 11am–4pm.*

and other live performances. They serve regional libations and hand-made Australian-style pies and other snacks. If you can, catch one of the regular tapings of *Live Wire! Radio*, a modern take on multi-performer vaudeville shows. 🕐 *1 hr. 3000 NE Alberta St. at 30th Ave.* ☎ *503/719-6055. www.albertarosetheatre.com. Showtimes vary & some performances are 21 & over only.*

⑧ ★★ McMenamins Kennedy School. Detention never sounded as appealing as it does at this 1912 grade school, renovated and reopened in 1997 as a combination hotel, restaurant, and movie theater. There are no less than five bars on the premises, including the Detention Bar, Honors Bar, and the Boiler Room, all serving beer and other alcoholic tipples from the on-site brewery. Thirty-five guest rooms fill former classrooms, and the walls are covered in original art and historical photos. Relax in the hot outdoor soaking pool or catch a matinee on a couch in the second-run movie theater. 🕐 *15 min. 5736 NE 33rd Ave.* ☎ *503/249-3983. www.mcmenamins.com.*

The restaurant at the remodeled Kennedy School, now a hotel.

⑦ ★ Alberta Rose Theatre.

Yet another lovingly resurrected old theater, the 300-seat Alberta Rose started as a motion picture house in 1927, operated until 1978, and was reborn as a space for independent films, comedy, acoustic music,

Southeast Portland:
Hawthorne & Belmont

1. Belmont District
2. Avalon Theater
3. Historic Belmont Firehouse
4. Tao of Tea
5. Central Hawthorne District
6. Bagdad Theater & Pub
7. Fat Straw
8. Mike's Movie Memorabilia Collection
9. Laurelhurst Park

The giant sunflower painted at the intersection of SE 33rd Avenue and Yamhill Street captures the friendly, community-minded spirit of this part of town, where downtown can seem a world away, even though it's just a 5-minute drive (or 15-minute bike ride) across the river. The vibe here is mostly laid-back and unpretentious (Hawthorne was the hippie haunt of Portland back in the 1960s and '70s), with tree-lined streets and sometimes as much bicycle traffic as cars and trucks. START: Bus 14 or 15.

① ★★ **Belmont District.** The commercial district on Southeast Belmont Street packs a lot into just a few blocks. You'll find shopping at eclectic places like **Noun** (3300 SE Belmont St. at 33rd Ave.), a quirky housewares/antiques store, and **Palace** (828 SE 34th Ave. at Belmont St.), with upscale new and vintage clothing for men and women. Hungry? Grab a great burger at **Dick's Kitchen** (3312 SE

Belmont St. at 33rd Ave.) and dessert at **Saint Cupcake,** which shares a storefront with Noun. Thirsty? **Stumptown Coffee Roasters** (3356 SE Belmont St. at 33rd Ave.) offers great people-watching, plus free coffee cuppings (aka tastings) daily at noon and 2pm in their Annex two doors down. For nightlife, try the Avalon Theater (see below) or head downstairs to **The Liquor Store** (3341 SE Belmont St. at 33rd

Quirky antiques and housewares at Noun on Belmont Street.

Ave.), which is not a real liquor store but a venue for jazz and blues. ⏱ *1 hr. SE Belmont St. from 33rd to 35th aves.*

② ★ **kids Avalon Theater.** Second-run movies and nickel arcade games—is there any better way to stretch your date dollars? Oregon's oldest theater (1912) was also the first in the state with more than one screen. Now it shows films on three screens and fills the rest of the space with Wunderland, an arcade of skee-ball, air hockey, and video games. You can even redeem your skee-ball tickets for prizes and candy. ⏱ *1 hr. 3451 SE Belmont St. at 34th Ave.* ☎ *503/238-1617. Sun–Fri noon–midnight, Sat 11am–midnight. Movies $4 adults, $3 seniors & children 11 & under. Arcade admission $3 adults, $2.50 children. Games 25¢.*

③ ★ **kids Historic Belmont Firehouse.** Kids and history buffs love this 1912 firehouse, now home to a safety learning center and museum dedicated to Portland's firefighting history. Restored antique gear and equipment, like an 1859 Jeffers Sidestroke Hand-pump Fire Engine, are on display and, often, touchable. There's even a fire pole to slide down! ⏱ *15 min. 900 SE 35th Ave. at 34th Ave.* ☎ *503/823-3615. www.jeffmorris-foundation.org. Open the 2nd Sat of every month, except July–Aug & Dec, 10am–3pm, or by appointment.*

Coffee is definitely Portland's caffeine of choice, but tea has become increasingly popular. One of the best spots for a freshly brewed cup of organic assam or Oolong is the **④** **Tao of Tea.** The teahouse also offers a nice selection of simple, vegetarian-friendly snacks and meals. *3430 SE Belmont St.* ☎ *503/736-0119. www.taooftea. com. $.*

⑤ ★★ **Central Hawthorne District.** It's hard to beat Hawthorne Boulevard from 34th to 39th avenues for strollable shopping, eating, and entertainment. The whole commercial stretch runs roughly from 30th to 50th avenues,

Saint Cupcake on Belmont Street.

with everything from brewpubs to vintage clothing stores. The heart of it is in the high 30s, especially the block between 36th and 37th avenues, where you'll find the historic **Bagdad Theater & Pub** (see below), a branch of **Powell's Books** (3723 SE Hawthorne Blvd. at 36th Ave.) specializing in home and garden titles, and **Pastaworks** (3735 SE Hawthorne Blvd. at 36th Ave.), a European-style grocery and deli

with an on-site eatery called **Evoe**. Other spots worth a stop are **Presents of Mind** (3633 SE Hawthorne Blvd. at 36th Ave.) for all things gift-oriented, **Imelda's Shoes and Louie's Shoes for Men** (3426 SE Hawthorne Blvd. at 34th Ave.), and **The Perfume House** (3328 SE Hawthorne Blvd.) for an outstanding selection of perfumes. ⏱ *2 hr. SE Hawthorne Blvd. btw. 34th & 39th aves.*

Imelda's Shoes on Hawthorne Boulevard.

6 ★★ Bagdad Theater & Pub. One of Portland's grandest old theaters is now the main anchor of the Hawthorne commercial district. You can see a movie or show inside, knock back a tipple at one of two bars (including one behind the screen), or enjoy a meal and craft-brewed beer at the restaurant, which spills out onto the sidewalk in good weather. The building itself is eye-popping inside, restored to the full opulence of its inauguration in 1927, minus the spouting fountain. *See p 42,* **9**.

The name **7 Fat Straw** will make sense when you order your first glass of "boba" (bubble tea), a milky Asian concoction with tapioca balls on the bottom. The less adventurous can go with fresh avocado or coconut-mango smoothies, or regular tea or coffee, and for noshing they serve tasty bánh mi (Vietnamese sandwiches). *4258 SE Hawthorne Blvd. at 42nd Ave.* ☎ *503/233-3369. www.fatstrawpdx. com. $.*

8 ★ Mike's Movie Memorabilia Collection. Ever wonder what happened to the knife from the shower scene in Hitchcock's *Psycho* or the monster costume from *Young Frankenstein?* They're here, inside the Movie Madness video store, along with other one-of-a-kind cinematic costumes and props. *See p 36,* **10**.

Feeding the ducks in Laurelhurst Park.

9 ★★ kids Laurelhurst Park. Sometimes all you need at the end of a good walk is a shady patch of grass, maybe with a playground for the kids or a duck pond nearby. Look no further—27-acre Laurelhurst Park has all these and more, including a picnic grove, a hillside of rhododendrons, and towering trees. Designed in 1909 by the Olmsted Brothers (sons of the man responsible for New York's Central Park), Laurelhurst became the first Portland city park to be listed on the National Register of Historic Places. There's an off-leash area for dogs and, across Stark Street, a children's playground next to tennis and basketball courts. (Originally, girls were supposed to play on the north side and boys on the south.) *See p 23,* **7**.

Inner Southeast

1. Vera Katz Eastbank Esplanade
2. Oregon Museum of Science and Industry
3. Springwater Corridor
4. Southeast Clinton Street
5. Dots Café
6. People's Food Co-op
7. Ladd's Addition
8. The Hat Museum
9. Cartopia
10. Kidd's Toy Museum

----- MAX Light Rail
----- Portland Streetcar

NE Multnomah St.

Holladay Park

LLOYD DISTRICT

Steel Br.

NE Lloyd Blvd.

84

Willamette R.

Burnside Br.

E Burnside St.

Sandy Blvd.

SE Stark St.

SE Martin Luther King Jr. Blvd.

SE 11th Ave.

Lone Fir Cemetery

BUCKMAN

SE Morrison St.

Morrison Br.

SE Belmont St.

BELMONT

Col. Summers Park

5

SE 7th Ave.

SE Madison St.

Hawthorne Br.

SE Grand Ave.

SE Hawthorne Blvd.

9

8

LADD'S ADDITION

7

SE 12th Ave.

Marquam Br.

2

Tilikum Crossing

SE Division St.

SE Clinton St.

5

4

SE 25th Ave.

SE 26th Ave.

6

3

Ross Island Br.

SE Powell Blvd.

SE McLoughlin Blvd.

Springwater Corridor

Brooklyn Park

BROOKLYN

SE Milwaukie Ave.

Powell Park

0   1/4 mi
0   1/4 km

Portland's inner Southeast district starts with the Central Eastside Industrial District near the river, but gives way to the mostly residential Hosford-Abernethy neighborhood. Cooperative gardens, alternative schools, and chicken coops (with real chickens, of course, but no roosters) are common sights around here. Small commercial hubs along Clinton and Division streets combine restaurants, coffee shops, and unique local businesses like Langlitz Leathers (2443 SE Division St.), creators of the first custom leather motorcycle jacket in 1947, and nearby Loprinzi's Gym (2414 SE 41st Ave.), an ultra-old-school bodybuilding facility. START: **Bus 4, 6, 10, 14, 15, 31, 32, or 33.**

❶ ★★ **kids** **Vera Katz Eastbank Esplanade.** Start on the east bank of the Willamette, where this paved path runs for 1½ miles from the Hawthorne Bridge to the Steel Bridge, with great river-level views of the city's downtown skyline. Along the trail you'll pass public art, map markers, and interpretive panels on the history of the river and the area. A 1,200-foot floating walkway, the longest of its kind in the country, leads under the Burnside Bridge and past a public boat dock. (If you have time, the entire 2-mile loop across the Steel and Hawthorne bridges and through Governor Tom McCall Waterfront Park is a Portland must-do.) The esplanade is named for German-born Vera Katz, who was the first woman to serve as the Speaker of the Oregon House of Representatives and was mayor of Portland from 1993 to 2005. ⏲ *30 min.*

❷ ★★ **kids** **Oregon Museum of Science and Industry.** At the southern end of the esplanade, "OMSI" boasts all the

Joggers and cyclists on the Eastbank Esplanade's floating walkway.

Hands-on chemistry at OMSI.

science-themed learning options you could ask for, from the hands-on exhibits, planetarium, and giant-screen theater inside to an actual submarine moored in the river. This end of the Eastbank Esplanade, under the Marquam Bridge that carries I-5, is particularly pretty on sunny days, with views of the Hawthorne Bridge and the South Waterfront. *See p 18,* **8**.

3 ★ **Springwater Corridor.** From OMSI, it's just a few blocks to the start of this 21-mile multiuse recreation trail that leads south and east through Sellwood to the town of Boring (seriously), part of a 40-mile paved loop that circles the entire city. It's worth exploring even just the beginning of the trail, which follows old trolley train tracks along the surprisingly green and quiet riverbank. *Note:* The restored Linneman Trolley Station near Southeast Powell and 185th is a convenient trailhead at which to park your car, fill your water bottles,

or use the public restrooms. Another handy Springwater pit stop is at Southeast 136th, where a small market serves up liquid refreshment. Another thing to note: In the past, Springwater Corridor has attracted the homeless and seen the erection and removal of tent cities. On my last visit before press time, it had been cleaned up. ⏱ *30 min.*

4 ★★ **Southeast Clinton Street.** The stretch of Clinton Street from 16th to 26th avenues definitely takes the prize for cutest street ramble in this part of town. It's dotted with local shops, cafes, bars, and restaurants, like the Swedish favorite **Bröder** (2508 SE Clinton St. at 25th Ave.; ☎ 503/736-3333), all without sacrificing its offbeat residential neighborhood vibe. The art-house **Clinton Street Theater** (2522 SE Clinton St. at 26th Ave.; ☎ 503/238-8899) has been showing the cult classic *The Rocky Horror Picture Show* every Saturday night since 1978, the longest run in the world. Beer lovers can even order a pint at the tiny attached brewpub and bring it into the theater with them. ⏱ *1 hr.*

One of Portland's best-loved dives, 5̲ **Dots Cafe** is famous for its authentically awful '60s decor of velvet paintings and Naugahyde-covered booths. Aesthetics aside, it's also a place where you can relax with a snack or light meal. *2521 SE Clinton St.* ☎ *503/235-0203. $.*

6̲ ★ **People's Food Co-op.** To experience Portland's fresh-local-seasonal-organic foodie mania in its purest essence—you know, the one behind all those "Know Your Farmer" bumper stickers—pop into this cooperative grocery store just south of Clinton Street. Whether it's local dairy products in glass bottles or hard-to-find bulk items like mulberries and jungle peanuts, they have it, along with prepackaged snack items, a fresh juice cart, and a year-round farmers' market out front every Wednesday. ⏱ *15 min. 3029 SE 21st Ave.* ☎ *503/674-2642. www.peoples.coop. Daily 8am–10pm.*

7̲ ★★★ **Ladd's Addition.** North of the Clinton neighborhood is one of the city's most distinctive residential districts, a diagonal grid extending from Division to Hawthorne streets and 12th to 20th avenues. The highlights for visitors, aside from the general serenity of the tree-lined streets, are the five rose gardens incorporated into its layout. A large central garden and four smaller diamond-shaped ones at the points of the compass are tended by neighborhood residents

and contain more than 3,000 roses. Ladd's Addition is the oldest planned community on the West Coast and contains wonderful examples of residential architecture from the late 1890s to the 1930s. *See p 23,* 5̲.

8̲ ★★ **The Hat Museum.** Tucked away in the Ladd-Reingold House, one of Ladd's Addition's older homes, is this incredible collection of chapeaus, a private labor of love that's one of the largest of its kind in the country. Some 1,300 hats date back to 1845 and include hats worn in the movies *Gangs of New York* and *Chicago.* A prearranged tour is required. *See p 36,* 9̲.

The food cart "pod" at SE Hawthorne Street and 12th Avenue aka 9̲ **Cartopia,** was one of the first to really take hold in Portland, and now has covered outdoor seating and an ATM. Take your pick from a vegan apple pie at **Whiffies Fried Pies** (☎ 503/946-6544), a freshly made wood-oven pizza at **Pyro Pizza** (☎ 503/929-1404), Belgian-style or poutine (fries with cheese curds and gravy) at **Potato Champion** (☎ 503/505-7086), or whichever of the other cart options strikes your fancy. *Hours vary, most carts open until 3am. $.*

🔟 ★ **kids Kidd's Toy Museum.** The last stop on this tour is another private collection, this time of vintage games and toys. Owner Frank Kidd is full of stories about the items featured in this multi-room display, which includes an astonishing array of cast-iron mechanical banks and more than a few cringe-inducing examples from the less-PC days of yore. *See p 36,* 8̲.

Sellwood

1 Oaks Bottom Wildlife Refuge
2 Oaks Amusement Park
3 Sellwood Riverfront Park
4 Jade Bistro and Patisserie
5 Antique Row

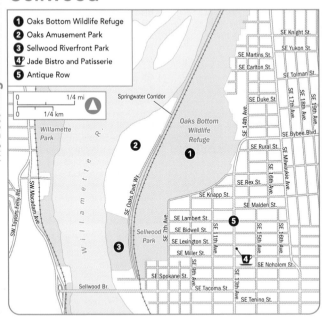

Once a separate city from Portland, Sellwood still feels more like a small village than a close-in Portland neighborhood. You don't have to take a passenger ferry to get to this old neighborhood on the east bank of the Willamette River, as folks did in the 19th century—you can even arrive by bike along the paved Springwater Corridor trail south from OMSI (4 miles, 20–25 min.). Most of Sellwood's boutiques, coffee shops, restaurants, and antiques stores are concentrated along SE Milwaukee Avenue and SE 13th Avenue. Otherwise, it's a homey neighborhood of bungalows and Victorian cottages, perfect for strolling, especially through the parks along the riverbank. START: Bus 70.

1 ★★ **Oaks Bottom Wildlife Refuge.** Two trails meander through this 141-acre flood-plain wetland on the east bank of the Willamette: a hiking trail along the river bluff, and the paved Springwater Corridor linking Sellwood and Portland's Eastbank Esplanade. The woodlands, pond, and meadows

are home to scores of birds, including quail, hawks, ducks, woodpeckers, and kestrels. You may spot some great blue herons (Portland's official city bird), too, since this former construction landfill is close to the Ross Island rookery. If you forgot your field guide, just look up—the huge hand-painted mural on

The Springwater Corridor links Sellwood to the Eastbank Esplanade.

the outside of the **Wilhelm Portland Memorial Mausoleum** (6705 SE 14th Ave.), visible from the refuge, portrays many of the birds that call Oaks Bottom home, including a great blue heron and an osprey. This 43,000-square-foot mural is likely the largest of its kind in the country. ⏱ *45 min. Parking lots & trailheads at SE Milwaukee Ave. & McLoughlin Blvd. & at SE 7th Ave. & Sellwood Blvd.* ☎ *503/823-6131. Daily 5am–midnight.*

❷ ★★★ kids Oaks Amusement Park. It's hard to decide who enjoys this historic amusement park more: the tots riding the historic carousel and miniature train, the teenagers screaming and laughing in the vintage roller rink, or the parents herding everyone around. Oaks is the oldest continually operating amusement park in the country, in business since 1905,

and it packs a lot into a little space on the bank of the Willamette, from the usual—carnival games, Ferris wheel, bumper cars—to the unique, including a 1912 carved carousel and large wooden roller-skating rink complete with pipe organ. *See p 31,* ❾.

❸ ★★ kids Sellwood Riverfront Park. Just south of Oaks Bottom at the base of the old Sellwood Bridge (a new Sellwood Bridge has just replaced it), this riverside park offers hiking trails, picnic tables, beach access, and a small wetland reserve at its north end. The open grassy part includes an off-leash area for dogs. Walk north along the riverbank a little ways for a good view of downtown Portland, and an enclave of houseboats. Free public concerts happen on Monday evenings in the summer. On the other side of SE Oaks Park Way (across the train tracks

Go-karting at the Oaks Amusement Park.

and Springwater Corridor), the larger **Sellwood Park** offers a swimming pool, sports fields and courts, and a playground. ⏱ *45 min. Entrance at SE Spokane St. & Oaks Pkwy. Daily 5am–midnight.*

A modern take on an Asian teahouse, 🐸 **Jade Bistro and Patisserie** offers a complete Vietnamese menu, but also a good selection of smaller bites such as baguette sandwiches, spicy green papaya salad, and, of course, lots and lots of teas. Desserts are a specialty, especially the Vietnamese Wedding Cake and chocolate-and-sea-salt French macaroons. *7912 SE 13th Ave.* ☎ *503/477-8985. www. jadeportland.com. $$.*

❺ ★ **Antique Row.** If there's one thing Sellwood is known for, it's antiquing in the vintage stores along SE 13th Avenue. You'll find all kinds of collectible memorabilia (and junk, too), housewares, jewelry, and more. It may take some digging to find your own particular treasure, **Sellwood Collective Antiques** (8027 SE 13th Ave. at Spokane St.) provides some good browsing opportunities. ⏱ *1 hr. Along SE 13th Ave., roughly btw. Malden & Tacoma sts.* ●

Downtown & Pearl District Shopping

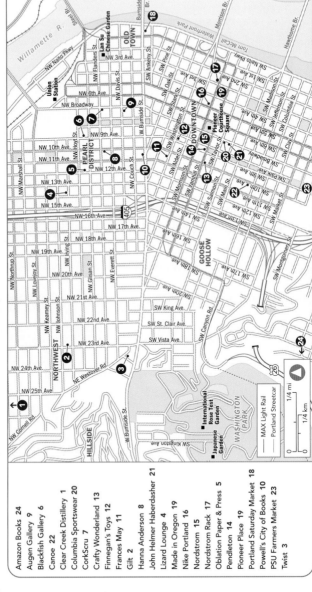

East Side Shopping

Amenity Shoes **4**	Grasshopper **2**
Ampersand Gallery & Fine Books **3**	Green Bean Books **1**
Barnes & Noble Booksellers **8**	Imelda's Shoes and Louie's Shoes for Men **18**
Broadway Books **7**	Lloyd Center **8**
Cargo **11**	Macy's **8**
Cosmic Monkey Comics **5**	Mink Boutique **15**
Fourteen 30 Contemporary **10**	Music Millennium **12**
Noun **13**	
The Perfume House **14**	
Presents of Mind **17**	
Red Light Clothing Exchange **16**	
Redux **9**	
Things from Another World **6**	

p 73: Furniture, Asian antiques, and more at Cargo.

Shopping Best Bets

Best for **Books**
★★★ Powell's City of Books,
1005 W. Burnside St. (p 78)

Best for **Shoes**
★★ Imelda's Shoes and Louie's
Shoes for Men, *3426 SE Hawthorne
Blvd. (p 80)*

Best for **Unexpected
Discoveries**
★★ Cargo, *81 SE Yamhill St.
(p 81)*

Best for **Toys**
★★★ Finnegan's Toys,
820 SW Washington St. (p 78)

Best for **Arty Surprises**
★★ Ampersand Vintage,
2916 NE Alberta St. Ste. B (p 77)

Best for **Handcrafted Gifts**
★★ Crafty Wonderland,
802 SW 10th Ave. (p 78)

Best for **Oregon Souvenirs**
★★ Made in Oregon,
Pioneer Place Mall (p 81)

Best for **Hats**
★★ John Helmer Haberdasher,
969 SW Broadway Ave. (p 80)

Best for **Kids' Clothes**
★★★ Hanna Andersson,
327 NW 10th Ave. (p 78)

Best for **Jewelry**
★★ Gilt, *720 NW 23rd Ave. (p 82)*

Best for **Sheer Selection**
★★ Pioneer Place,
700 SW 5th Ave. (p 82)

Best for **Used Outfits**
★ Red Light Clothing Exchange,
3590 SE Hawthorne Blvd. (p 81)

Best for **Records & CDs**
★★★ Music Millennium,
3158 E. Burnside St. (p 83)

Best for **Fragrances**
★★★ The Perfume House,
3328 SE Hawthorne Blvd. (p 78)

Best to **Satisfy Your Inner
Anime**
★★ Things From Another World,
2916 NE Broadway. (p 78); and ★★
Cosmic Monkey Comics,
5335 NE Sandy Blvd. (p 77)

Best **Fresh, Local, Sustainable,
Organic Produce Selection**
★★★ PSU Farmers Market,
*SW Park Ave. at SW Montgomery St.
(p 82)*

Shoppers peruse the shelves at Powell's City of Books.

Portland Shopping A to Z

Art

★★★ **Augen Gallery** DOWN-TOWN   One of Portland's older galleries shows paintings and prints by regional artists and printmakers; their Pearl gallery (817 SW 2nd Ave.; ☎ 503/224-8182) specializes in prints. *716 NW Davis St. (at 7th Ave.). ☎ 503/546-5056. www. augengallery.com. Bus: 15 or 51. Map p 74.*

★★ **Blackfish Gallery** PEARL This artist-owned cooperative isn't afraid to push the envelope, showing contemporary images as well as mixed-media pieces by lesser-known artists. *420 NW 9th Ave. (at Flanders St.). ☎ 503/224-2634. www.blackfish.com. Streetcar: NW 10th & Glisan; Bus: 17. Map p 74.*

★ **Fourteen 30 Contemporary** SOUTHWEST   Step inside this immaculate white space to find works by artists on the cusp of breaking big. Often shows video and sculpture too, unusual for Portland. *1501 SW Market St. ☎ 503/ 236-1430. www.fourteen30.com. MAX: Goose Hollow/SW Jefferson St. Map p 75.*

Books, Magazines & Comics

★★ **Amazon Books** BEAVERTON Amazon's first brick-and-mortar store in the Portland area carries a selective inventory based on sales trends and reviews from the retail giant's online division. *9585 SW Washington Square Dr. ☎ 503/620-9933. www.amazon.com. BUS: 45. Map p 74.*

★★ **Ampersand Gallery & Fine Books** ALBERTA   Are fine and offbeat antique books and images your thing? Come here for books of photography, botanical cyanotypes, old mug shot photographs, 1920s erotica, and 1950s illustrated car owner's manuals. There's also a monthly art exhibition. *2916 NE Alberta St. Ste. B (at 29th Ave.). ☎ 503/805-5458. www. ampersandgallerypdx.com. Bus: 72. Map p 75.*

★★★ **Barnes & Noble Booksellers** LLOYD CENTER   Barnes & Noble Lloyd Center branch is a big, browsable bookstore with a great selection of current bestsellers and still-in-print titles in all genres. There's another B&N at Clackamas Town Center Mall, 12000 SE 82nd Ave. (☎ 503/788-3464). Both stores host regular author events, book signings, and book groups. *1317 Lloyd Center. www.bn.com. ☎ 503/ 249-0800. MAX: Lloyd Center. Map p 75.*

★★ **Broadway Books** NORTH-EAST   At this quintessential neighborhood bookstore, the owners have an excellent eye for titles and are happy to point you to just the right book. *1714 NE Broadway Ave. (at 17th St.). ☎ 503/284-1726. www. broadwaybooks.net. Bus: 9 or 77. Map p 75.*

★★ **Cosmic Monkey Comics** NORTHEAST   No matter what you're after—anime, manga, graphic novels, or the latest titles— you'll find it here at Portland's premier comics store. Don't miss the back room, full of back issues and trades. *5335 NE Sandy Blvd. (at Sandycrest Terrace). ☎ 503/517-9050. www.cosmicmonkeycomics.com. Bus: 12. Map p 75.*

★ **Green Bean Books** ALBERTA Imagine the ideal children's bookstore: new and used books in a colorful space, comfy couches, and even a draping shady tree out back to read under. That's Green Bean

Books. *1600 NE Alberta St. (at 16th Ave.).* ☎ *503/954-2354. www.green beanbookspdx.com. Bus: 72. Map p 75.*

★★★ Powell's City of Books

PEARL What can you say about the world's best and largest independent bookstore, a full city block of literature? Don't visit Portland without popping in at Powell's. *1005 W. Burnside St. (at 10th Ave.).* ☎ *503/228-4651. www.powells.com. Bus: 20; Streetcar: NW 10th & Couch. Map p 74.*

★★ Things From Another World

HOLLYWOOD Fanboys rejoice! Not just wall-to-wall comics, but also collectible toys, figurines, games, and a couch for perusing. *2916 NE Broadway.* ☎ *503/284-2693. www.tfaw.com. Bus: 17. Map p 75.*

Children's Clothing & Toys

★★★ Finnegan's Toys

DOWNTOWN This über-toy store with an emphasis on learning and quality over screens and cheap junk is fun for adults as well as kids. *820 SW Washington St.* ☎ *503/221-0306. www.finneganstoys.com. Streetcar: Central Library; MAX: Library/SW 9th Ave. Map p 74.*

★★ Grasshopper

ALBERTA Handmade children's clothes, European toys, and award-winning books—this place is enough to make you want kids if you don't have them already. *1816 NE Alberta St. (at 18th Ave.).* ☎ *503/335-3131. www.grasshopperstore.com. Bus: 72. Map p 75.*

★★★ Hanna Andersson

PEARL Children's clothes get a sunny Swedish makeover from this well-known local designer. Her shop is like catnip to grandparents, but the kids love it, too. *327 NW 10th Ave. (at Flanders St.).* ☎ *503/ 321-5275. www.hannaanderson.com.*

Streetcar: NW 11th & Everett; Bus: 17. Map p 74.

Cosmetics & Perfumes

★★★ The Perfume House

HAWTHORNE Owner Chris Tsefalas, one of only 26 official "Noses" in the world, will help you discover your own special fragrance in this unique shop located in a house. *3328 SE Hawthorne Blvd. (at 33rd Ave.).* ☎ *503/234-5375. www.the perfumehouse.com. Bus: 14. Map p 75.*

Crafts

★★ Crafty Wonderland

DOWNTOWN What started as a temporary "pop-up shop" is now a permanent home to works by more than 90 talented local artisans, purveying cards, clothing, soap, pins, and all kinds of other handcrafted treasures. *802 SW 10th Ave. (at Yamhill St.).* ☎ *503/224-9097. www. craftywonderland.com. Streetcar: Central Library. Map p 74.*

★★ Portland Saturday Market

OLD TOWN Every Saturday and Sunday from March through

Local artists are featured at Crafty Wonderland.

December, some 300 craftspeople and artisans set up shop outdoors under the west end of the Burnside Bridge. Food and free entertainment round out the fun. *W. Burnside Ave. btw. SW 1st Ave. & SW Naito Pkwy.* ☎ *503/222-6072. www.portlandsaturdaymarket.com. MAX: Skidmore Fountain; Bus: 16. Map p 74.*

★★★ **Twist** NORTHWEST True to its name, this boutique gallery carries creative housewares and handmade jewelry, and everything is just a little bit out of the ordinary—in a good way. *30 NW 23rd Place (at Westover Rd.).* ☎ *503/224-0334. www.twistonline.com. (Also at Pioneer Place Shopping Center, 700 SW 5th Ave.;* ☎ *503/222-3137.) Bus: 15 or 18. Map p 74.*

Department Stores
★★ **Macy's** LLOYD CENTER Alas, like so many other department stores, Macy's closed its downtown Portland store in 2017. But there's still an easy-to-reach Macy's store on the east side at Lloyd Center. Macy's is, well, Macy's, with clothing, accessories, housewares, makeup, linens, and more. *1001 Lloyd Center.* ☎ *503/281-4797. www.macyscom. MAX: Lloyd Center. Bus: 8. Map p 75.*

★★★ **Nordstrom** DOWNTOWN The only remaining department store in downtown Portland, Nordstrom on Pioneer Square offers the highest-quality designer clothing for men and women and is famed for its shoe departments. For great deals, try nearby **Nordstrom Rack** (245 SW Morrison St.). *701 SW Broadway Ave. (at Morrison St.).* ☎ *503/224-6666. www.nordstrom.com. (Also at 1001 Lloyd Center;* ☎ *503/287-2444.) Pioneer Sq. Map p 74.*

Fashion
★★ **Amenity Shoes** NORTHEAST Chic shoes (for both sexes) and bags in the Beaumont-Wilshire neighborhood. Many unique styles. *3430 NE 41st Ave. (at Fremont St.).* ☎ *503/282-4555. www.amenityshoes.com. Bus: 24 or 75. Map p 75.*

★★★ **Frances May** DOWNTOWN Quite possibly the city's top boutique for women's, men's, and kid's clothing, with high-end brands befitting New York or Los

The top boutique Francis May.

Farmers Markets

The Portland metro area supports no fewer than seven seasonal open-air farmers markets (www.portlandfarmersmarket.org). Along with farm-fresh produce and meats, you'll often find food carts, live music, and more.

- **Pioneer Courthouse Square Market:** SW Broadway & SW Morrison Street, Mondays June–September 10am–2pm.
- **Shemanski Park Market:** SW Park Avenue at SW Salmon Street, Wednesdays May–October, 10am–2pm.
- **Northwest Market:** NW 19th Avenue at NW Everett Street, Thursdays June–September, 2–6pm.
- **Buckman Market:** SF Salmon Street at 20th Avenue, Thursdays May–September, 3–7pm.
- **Portland State University Market:** Saturdays March–December, 8:30am–2pm.

Produce shopping at the PSU Farmers Market.

- **King Market:** NE 7th Avenue at NE Wygant Street, Sundays May–October, 10am–2pm.
- **Kenton Market:** N. McClellan & N. Denver Street, Fridays June–September, 3–7pm.

Angeles. *1003 SW Washington St. (at 10th Ave.).* ☎ *503/227-3402. www.francesmay.com. Streetcar: SW 10th & Stark; Bus: 15 or 51. Map p 74.*

★★★ **Imelda's Shoes and Louie's Shoes for Men** HAWTHORNE Boots, high heels, Mary Janes: If they're stylish and go on your feet, they have 'em here, even though you might have to save up. *3426 SE Hawthorne Blvd.* ☎ *503/233-7476. www.imeldasandlouies.com. Bus: 14. Map p 75.*

★★★ **John Helmer Haberdasher** DOWNTOWN Hankering for a hat? Craving a chapeau? John Helmer has been selling everything from fezzes to fedoras since 1921. This is one of Portland's great old stores. *969 SW Broadway Ave. (at Salmon St.).* ☎ *503/223-4976. www. johnhelmer.com. Bus: 15 or 51. Map p 74.*

★★ **Lizard Lounge** PEARL Hip duds for men and women, including sustainable local brand Nau and national ones like Billabong and Ray-Ban. And a ping-pong table. *1323 NW Irving St. (at 14th Ave.).* ☎ *503/416-7476. www.lizard loungepdx.com. Bus: 17. Map p 74.*

★★★ Mink Boutique HAW-
THORNE Adorable dresses, sassy skirts, and fit-like-a-glove jeans— plus jewelry, accessories, and a friendly, knowledgeable sales staff—make this a neighborhood favorite. *3418 SE Hawthorne Blvd. (at 34th Ave.).* ☎ *503/232-3500. www.shopmink.com. Bus: 14. Map p 75.*

★★★ Pendleton DOWNTOWN
Outfit yourself against the damp chill with fine wool fashions from this Northwest institution, and grab one of their famous woolen blankets for home. *825 SW Yamhill St.* ☎ *503/242-0037. www.pendleton-usa.com. MAX: Pioneer Courthouse Sq. Map p 74.*

★ Red Light Clothing Exchange HAWTHORNE Vintage
clothes are de rigueur to a certain stripe of Portlander, and this place has one of the biggest selections in town. *3590 SE Hawthorne Blvd. (at 36th Ave.).* ☎ *503/963-8888. www.redlightclothingexchange.com. Bus: 14. Map p 75.*

Gifts & Souvenirs
★★ Made in Oregon DOWN-
TOWN The full bounty of the Beaver State in one place—Tillamook cheese, Pendleton blankets, Timbers jerseys, Willamette pinots— make this the go-to place for local gifts. *Pioneer Place Mall, 340 SW Morrison St.* ☎ *503/241-3630. Also in the airport (*☎ *503/282-7827); and in Lloyd Center Mall, 1017 Lloyd Center (*☎ *503/282-7636). www.madeinoregon.com. MAX: Morrison/SW 3rd Ave. Map p 74.*

★★ Presents of Mind HAW-
THORNE Locally made jewelry, witty cards, and offbeat gifts make this an all-in-one gift-shopping destination. *3633 SE Hawthorne Blvd. (at 36th Ave.).* ☎ *503/230-7740. www.presentsofmind.tv. Bus: 14. Map p 75.*

Housewares
★★★ Canoe DOWNTOWN
This modern and carefully curated home store is dedicated to good contemporary design and is great for thoughtful gifts, from kitchen items to home furnishings. *1233 SW 12th Ave.* ☎ *503/889-8545. www.canoeonline.net. Streetcar: SW 11th & Alder; Bus: 15 or 51. Map p 74.*

★★ Cargo SOUTHEAST You'll
feel like you've stumbled into a Chinese warehouse during a festival at this kaleidoscopic place, full of furniture, Asian antiques, paper lanterns, jewelry, and other sundries. *81 SE Yamhill St.* ☎ *503/209-8349. www.cargoinc.com. Streetcar: SE M L King & Morrison; Bus: 6. Map p 75.*

★★ Noun BELMONT The per-
fect spot for tasteful packrats to

Artisan jewelry at Noun.

shop, this eastside nook carries charming antiques, artisan jewelry, and handmade stationery—plus you enter through a cupcake shop. *3300 SE Belmont St. (at 33rd Ave.). ☎ 503/235-0078. www.shopnoun. com. Bus: 15. Map p 75.*

Jewelry & Accessories

★★ **Gilt** NORTHWEST A perennial favorite for its vintage and locally designed jewelry, including many one-of-a-kind items. It's hard to leave empty-handed. *720 NW 23rd Ave. (at Johnson St.). ☎ 503/ 226-0629. www.gilt.com. Bus: 15. Map p 74.*

★★ **Redux** SOUTHEAST Everything in here used to be something else—all the wallets, belt buckles, ties, and jewelry are made of repurposed materials, often to charming and creative effect. *811 E. Burnside St. #110. ☎ 503/231-7336. www. reduxpdx.com. Bus: 12, 19, or 20. Map p 75.*

Malls & Markets

★★ **Lloyd Center** NORTHEAST The biggest and oldest shopping mall in the state has more than 100 stores, a multiplex movie theater, a food court, and even a famous indoor ice rink. *Btw. NE Multnomah & NE Halsey sts., from 9th to 13th aves. ☎ 503/282-2511. www.lloyd-center.com. MAX: Lloyd Center/NE 11th Ave.; Bus: 8, 9, 70, 73, or 77. Map p 75.*

★★ **Pioneer Place** DOWNTOWN The most fashionable shopping center in downtown, Pioneer Place has everything from an Apple Store to Victoria's Secret, plus a Regal cinema and a food court. *700 SW 5th Ave. (at Morrison St.). ☎ 503/ 228-5800. www.pioneerplace.com. MAX: Mall/SW 4th Ave.; Bus: 1, 8, 12, or 94. Map p 74.*

★★★ **PSU Farmers Market** DOWNTOWN The biggest and

Downtown's fashionable Pioneer Place Mall.

Lucinda Williams performs in-store at Music Millennium.

by far most popular of Portland's seven seasonal open-air markets, the one at PSU fills two full park blocks with fresh-off-the-farm produce, flowers, cheese, wine, meat, seafood, and other goodies. *SW Park Ave. at SW Montgomery St.* ☎ *503/241-0032. www.portland farmersmarket.org. Free admission. Streetcar: SW Park & Mill. Map p 74.*

Music/CDs
★★★ Music Millennium

LAURELHURST Think of it as the musical equivalent of Powell's Books, only way more funky: a vast library of new and used CDs in every genre, including classical, some rare treasures, an extensive vinyl section, plus in-store performances. Music Millennium has been around forever and is one of Portland's great old stores. *3158 E. Burnside St. (at 32nd Ave.).* ☎ *503/ 231-8926. www.musicmillennium. com. Bus: 20. Map p 75.*

Sportswear
★★★ Columbia Sportswear

DOWNTOWN This local sportswear giant's flagship store brims with ruggedly fashionable gear designed to last. Prices are lower at the factory outlet in Sellwood (1323 SE Tacoma St.; ☎ 503/238-0118). *911 SW Broadway Ave. (at Taylor St.).* ☎ *503/226-6800. www. columbia.com. MAX: Library/SW 9th Ave.; Bus: 15 or 51. Map p 74.*

★★★ Nike Portland DOWN-

TOWN A temple to athletic performance (and the clothing thereof); fitting, because Nike got its start here. The outlet (2650 NE Martin Luther King Jr. Blvd.; ☎ 503/281-5901) has deals on last year's lines. *638 SW 5th Ave.* ☎ *503/221-6453. www.nike.com. MAX: Pioneer Sq. Map p 74.*

Stationery & Cards
★★ Oblation Papers & Press

PEARL Unique, high-quality stationery, cards, wedding invites, and

Pear eau de vie at Clear Creek Distillery.

Wines & Spirits
★★★ Clear Creek Distillery

NORTHWEST Combine European brandy-making techniques with Oregon fruit and you get unbeatable eaux de vie, grappa, wine brandy, and fruit liqueurs, all of which you can sample here. *2389 NW Wilson St. (at 24th Ave.).* ☎ *503/248-9470. www.clearcreek distillery.com. Bus: 15, 17, or 77. Map p 74.*

CorkScru PEARL These guys know their vintages, especially sub-$12 values, and they specialize in wine six-packs from Italy, France, and, of course, Oregon. *339 NW Broadway (at Flanders St.).* ☎ *503/226-9463. www.corkscru.biz. Bus: 9, 17. Map p 74.* ●

the like made on handmade paper with century-old letterpresses. *516 NW 12th Ave. (at Hoyt St.).* ☎ *503/223-1093. www.oblation papers.com. Streetcar: NW 11th & Glisan. Map p 74.*

Forest **Park**

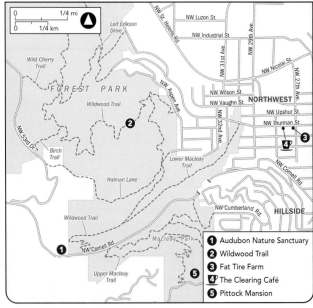

1 Audubon Nature Sanctuary
2 Wildwood Trail
3 Fat Tire Farm
4 The Clearing Café
5 Pittock Mansion

Extending west for 8 miles from the heart of Portland's West Hills, Forest Park points like a lush green finger toward the mouth of the Columbia River. At 5,100 acres, it's the largest urban forest in the nation, with 8 square miles of fern-filled ravines, rushing streams, and towering firs, cedars, maples, and alders. The city's green playground is spiderwebbed with more than 80 miles of trails and fire lanes for hiking, biking, and running, and it is home to over 112 bird and 62 mammal species. There's no visitor center or main entrance; instead, at least 17 access points circle the park edge. (One main gateway is the start of Leif Erikson Drive, a 12-mile gravel road, at the end of NW Thurman St.) The west end of the park, away from downtown, is much wilder than the more heavily visited eastern end. Note: Dogs must be kept on leashes throughout Forest Park. START: **Drive to 5151 NW Cornell Rd.**

1 ★★ kids **Audubon Nature Sanctuary.** Tucked up against Forest Park's southern side, this wildlife rehabilitation center is home to all kinds of injured critters

being nursed back to health (or simply given a place to live), from coyotes to bald eagles. Sometimes they'll bring the animals out for up-close encounters. There's a gift

Previous page: The lovely International Rose Test Garden.

Running in Forest Park.

shop and 150 acres of forest with a few miles of trails, including a newt-filled pond. It's also a good starting point for the Wildwood and Upper MacLeay trails in Forest Park proper. *See p 22,* ❷.

❷ ★★★ **Wildwood Trail.** Forest Park's longest trail is 27 sinuous miles of fern-lined curves, stream crossings, and switchbacks (plus another three in Washington Park). This National Recreation Trail is marked by blue diamonds and mile markers every quarter mile, which make it easy to take it in pieces; almost every loop hike in the park involves the Wildwood. Its eastern end sees a good bit of foot traffic, while its west end is in the wilder western part of the park.

❸ ★ **Fat Tire Farm.** Close to 30 miles of fire roads in Forest Park are open to mountain bikers. (Hiking trails are not.) If you want to try mountain biking, head to this bike shop 1 mile down Thurman Street from the Leif Erickson Drive entrance, and rent a high-end mountain bike for the day. *2714 NW Thurman St. (at 27th Ave.).* ☎ *503/222-3276. www.fattirefarm. com. Bikes are $50–$200 for 24 hr. Mon–Fri 11am–7pm, Sat 10am–6pm, Sun noon–5pm.*

Fuel up for your hike (or recover afterward) with the healthy soups, panini, and tasty rice-and-bean bowls at ❹ **The Clearing Café** downhill from the Leif Erikson Drive entrance. *2772 NW Thurman St. (at 27th Ave.).* ☎ *503/841-6240. www. theclearingcafe.com. $.*

❺ ★★★ **Pittock Mansion.** You can reach this National Historic Landmark, perched 1,000 feet above Northwest Portland on a spur of Forest Park, via the Wildwood Trail (it's well worth the climb), by the 20 bus up W. Burnside, or by car (look for the turn-off on W. Burnside). Henry Pittock and his wife Georgiana, both first-generation Oregon immigrants, built this 23-room French Renaissance-style chateau in 1914, by which time Henry had become one of the most powerful men in Oregon. You can tour the interior or just enjoy the grounds, gardens, and views of Mt. Hood—first climbed by Pittock and four friends in 1854.

Washington **Park**

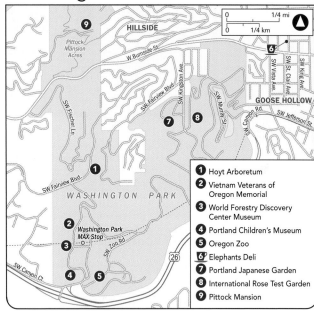

1 Hoyt Arboretum
2 Vietnam Veterans of Oregon Memorial
3 World Forestry Discovery Center Museum
4 Portland Children's Museum
5 Oregon Zoo
6 Elephants Deli
7 Portland Japanese Garden
8 International Rose Test Garden
9 Pittock Mansion

Closer to downtown, Washington Park is Forest Park's more urbane neighbor. It covers 410 acres of wooded hills between West Burnside Street and U.S. 26. It's basically an extension of the same forested landscape that characterizes Forest Park, albeit with more developed attractions in a smaller space. The park's 15-plus miles of trails, winding up and through the Hoyt Arboretum, are popular with hikers and joggers year-round. A shuttle bus runs from the Washington Park MAX station (the deepest transit station in North America, at 260 ft. down) to the Japanese and rose gardens and the arboretum (daily June–Sept, and on weekends in May and Oct). Note: Dogs must be kept on leashes throughout Washington Park. START: **MAX Washington Park; Bus 63 on weekdays only.**

1 ★★★ **Hoyt Arboretum.** This 187-acre reserve is much more than a woodsy park—it's a living museum of plants, with more than 8,000 shrubs and trees representing over 1,000 species from around the world, including dozens of species that are endangered in the wild. The trees are organized and grouped according to genus. There are always seasonal highlights, from the magnificent magnolias in the spring to fiery-colored maples in the fall and witch hazels in

Exploring Hoyt Arboretum.

mid-winter. I love the giant dawn redwoods, rare deciduous trees dating from the Jurassic period and thought to be extinct until specimens were discovered in China in the 1940s. Twelve miles of hiking trails wind through the arboretum, including the Wildwood Trail (p 87, ❷) that continues into Forest Park. At the visitor center, you can pick up maps for suggested routes of 1, 2, or 4 miles; 90-minute guided tours are offered on Saturdays at noon spring through fall. *Visitor Center: 4000 SW Fairview Blvd.* ☎ *503/865-8733. www.hoyt arboretum.org. Free admission; guided tours $3 per person, Apr–Oct Sat. Visitor center Mon–Fri 9am–4pm; Sat–Sun 11am–3pm. Grounds daily 6am–10pm. MAX: Washington Park. Bus: 63 on weekdays only.*

❷ ★ **Vietnam Veterans of Oregon Memorial.** On the south edge of the arboretum, this monument centers on a curved wall of black granite listing the names of Oregonians who died or went missing in action in Vietnam. A spiral path leads past smaller walls with narratives from the conflict contrasted with local events. *4000 SW Canyon Rd. Daily 5am–10pm. MAX: Washington Park. Bus: 63 on weekdays only.*

❸ ★ **kids** **World Forestry Center Discovery Museum.** The timber industry's major role in the development of the Pacific Northwest is the focus of this interactive museum geared mostly toward kids. Learn about the creatures that live under the forest floor, and ride into the (simulated) canopy of the Amazon rainforest. Out front sits "Peggy," a 33½-ton locomotive built in 1909, that hauled a billion feet of logs, more or less, in a 41-year career. *See p 22, ❸.*

❹ ★★ **kids** **Portland Children's Museum.** Are the tykes tired of trees? The Children's Museum isn't huge, but it packs a lot into a modest space: a treehouse for story time, a studio for making art from recycled materials, a miniature grocery store complete with shopping carts and scanners. Kids 8 and under or so will love this place. Traveling exhibits, classes, and visiting artists, musicians, and storytellers mean there's always something new. *See p 27, ❷.*

❺ ★★★ **kids** **Oregon Zoo.** I have to admit that I am not a fan of zoos, but this is a good one—and it's also the most popular attraction in the state. Kids love it. Felines, canines, primates, and pachyderms roam the habitats that cover 64 acres. Successful breeding programs for Asian elephants and

A lion at the Oregon Zoo.

California condors are the backbone of the zoo's conservation efforts. Popular seasonal events include a summer open-air concert series and a winter holiday light show, best viewed from the ⅝-scale steam train that chugs as far as the Japanese and Rose Test gardens. *See p 15,* ❷.

No relation to the zoo, the ❻ **Elephants Deli** just outside the park and back downtown has wood-fired pizza, grilled sandwiches, and a perennially tempting dessert case. Try the garlic fries or a salad from the cold case. *115 NW 22nd Ave. (at Davis St.).* ☎ *503/299-6304. $$.*

❼ ★★★ **Portland Japanese Garden.** Near the top of Portland's must-see list is this tranquil oasis of stone paths, koi ponds, and manicured trees and shrubs. Opened in 1967, the PJG is considered to be the most authentic Japanese garden outside of Japan. A new entrance area, a contemporary teahouse, and striking gallery buildings by Japanese architect Kengo Kuma opened in 2017. *See p 15,* ❶.

❽ ★★★ **International Rose Test Garden.** Portland's century-old floral showpiece was conceived and first planted during World War I, when local rosarians feared the bombs raining down on Europe might destroy entire rose species. Today this official rose test garden is home to about 10,000 blooming bushes of every conceivable variety, with a focus on award-winning hybrids. From June through September it's one endless photo op. Kids may not be thrilled by rows upon rows of roses, but just down SW Kingston Avenue is the **Rose Garden Children's Park,** a sprawling playground next to a picnic shelter in the zoo's old elephant barn. *See p 13,* ❿.

❾ ★★★ **Pittock Mansion.** While not technically in Washington Park, the mansion owned by Portland pioneer Henry Pittock is just across West Burnside Avenue (be careful crossing!) via the Wildwood Trail, and it's well worth a detour.

A Rose City by Any Other Name?

Portland can thank Leo Samuel, founder of Standard Insurance, for its flowery nickname. And while we're bestowing thanks, let's hear it for Georgiana Pittock, wife of the publisher of *The Oregonian* and builder of Pittock Mansion (see Forest Park, above, ⑤, or see ⑨, below for first popularizing roses in the late 19th century and helping to found the first Rose Festival in 1917. Leo Samuel, like Georgiana, was an enthusiastic rose gardener who would leave clippers by his bushes so that other people could help themselves to blossoms. Other gardeners followed suit, and word soon spread that weather and soil conditions in the city on the Willamette were ideal for these temperamental flowers. Roses are still grown on the grounds of Pittock Mansion in Forest Park and outside the Standard Insurance Company's home office on SW 6th Avenue between Salmon and Taylor streets downtown. Portland's other nickname, "Stumptown," comes from—you guessed it—the logging industry, while the popular shorthand PDX comes from the airline code for Portland International Airport.

Henry and his wife, Georgiana, both first-generation Oregon immigrants, built this 23-room home in 1914 and lived in it until they died. Perched 1,000 feet above the city, the house incorporates English, French, and Turkish designs but was built by Oregon craftsmen using Northwest materials. You can tour the interior or just enjoy the grounds, gardens, and views of Mount Hood—first climbed by Pittock and four friends in 1854. See p 12, ⑨.

Relaxing on the lawn outside the Pittock Mansion.

Portland **by Bike**

1. Waterfront Bicycle Rentals
2. Travel Portland Visitor Information Center
3. Courier Coffee Bar
4. Governor Tom McCall Waterfront Park
5. Hawthorne Bridge
6. Vera Katz Eastbank Esplanade
7. Springwater Corridor
8. Clinton Neighborhood
9. Tilikum Crossing Bridge
10. Hopworks BikeBar
11. Steel Bridge

MAX Light Rail
Portland Streetcar

t's official: Portland is the most bike-crazy city in the country, with the highest percentage of cycling commuters (around 7%), some 315 miles of bikeways and bike lanes, and annual bike-related events like the 2-week Pedalpalooza every June. At last count, the city boasted more than 30 artisan bike builders, a dozen bike clothing manufacturers, and some 75 bicycle sales/repair shops. And in 2016 it started BIKETOWN, a bike-sharing program (see below). This rolling tour offers a taste of what cycling in the City of Roses is all about. (*A word of caution:* Always wear a helmet.) START: **MAX Oak/SW 1st Ave.; Bus 16.**

1 ★★ Waterfront Bicycle Rentals. Didn't bring your own wheels? BIKETOWN (see above) is great for short hops on standard-issue bikes. If you want to rent a hybrid city-ready bike, a kid's bike, or a tandem for a longer period of time, this is a good place to do it. All rentals include a helmet, lock, map, and light; you can buy bike accessories, too. *10 SW Ash St. #100 (at Naito Pkwy.).* ☎ *503/227-1719.*

www.waterfrontbikes.com. Daily 10am–6pm. Rentals $9/hr. $28/half-day, $40/24 hr., $100/week.

2 ★★★ Travel Portland Visitor Information Center. If you did bring your own bike, or if you just need a little more guidance (and a super-handy *Bike There!* map), head to Pioneer Courthouse Square for some in-person riding advice. Odds are, whoever's behind the counter got there on two

Getting Around Stumptown with BIKETOWN

BIKETOWN, launched in 2016, is Portland's bikeshare program, designed for taking quick trips around downtown and close-in neighborhoods on the west and east side. The bright orange bike stations are located in busy areas throughout the Portland core. **BIKETOWN** (www.biketownpdx.com) offers three payment options: a single 30-minute ride for $2.50, a day pass including 180 minutes of ride time for $12, and an annual pass with 90 minutes of ride time per day for $12/month. The plans are available for purchase through the website, the mobile app, or at a station kiosk. At the station, you enter the pin number you received with sign-up or hold your member card above the touch pad, remove the lock, ride the bike, and return it to an open space at any other bike station. It's fun and simple, but it does not include a helmet.

wheels him- or herself that morning. *701 SW 6th Ave., Pioneer Courthouse Sq.* ☎ *503/275-8355. www.travelportland.com. Mon–Fri 8:30am–5:30pm, Sat 10am–4pm; May–Oct Sun 10am–2pm.*

Time for some leg gasoline—sorry, caffeine—at this fittingly cycle-centric little coffee roaster and cafe, **3 Courier Coffee Bar.** (They deliver their beans all over town—by bike, of course.) *923 SW Oak St.* ☎ *503/545-6444. $.*

4 ★★★ Governor Tom McCall Waterfront Park. If you only ride one place in town, it should be through this skinny park along the Willamette. It makes a great start for longer rides as well. Stretching from the Steel Bridge almost to the Marquam (I-5) bridge, it passes fountains, cherry trees, the Saturday Market, and the 1947 stern-wheeler *Portland* (home to the **Oregon Maritime Museum;** see p 53). It's also one segment of a popular 3-mile loop that crosses the Steel and Hawthorne bridges to

A cyclist on the bike-friendly Hawthorne Bridge.

the Eastbank Esplanade (see below). See p 9, ❷.

❺ ★★★ Hawthorne Bridge.
Cross the river on the country's oldest vertical-lift bridge, opened in 1910 and made bike-friendly in 1999 with wide sidewalks on both sides. Now it's Oregon's busiest bicycle bridge, with some 5,000 riders rolling across every day.

❻ ★★★ Vera Katz Eastbank Esplanade.
Opened in 2001, this 1.5-mile bike and walking trail (named for former Mayor Vera Katz) links the Steel and Hawthorne bridges on the east bank of the Willamette. It crosses a 1,200-foot floating walkway under the Burnside Bridge and is one of the best places to see Portland's skyline in all its riparian glory. See p 67, ❶.

❼ ★★ Springwater Corridor.
Once the track for a railroad that hauled passengers and produce, this 21-mile paved trail leads south from the Hawthorne Bridge and OMSI to the Sellwood neighborhood, home to Oaks Bottom Wildlife Refuge and Oaks Amusement Park. It's 4 miles to Sellwood, a scenic out-and-back ride along the river. From there, the trail turns east as part of the 40-mile loop around most of Portland (www.40mileloop.org). See p 68, ❸.

❽ ★★ Clinton Neighborhood.
After a detour down the Springwater Corridor and back, head east to this quintessential cycling neighborhood along SE Clinton Street and its popular bike path. There are dozens of places to eat, drink, and shop, concentrated around SE 21st and 26th avenues and at the "Seven Corners" intersection of SE Division Street and SE 20th Avenue. Look for the huge wheel of the

penny-farthing outside **A Better Cycle** (2324 SE Division St.; ☎ 503/265-8595), a worker-owned bike shop. See p 68, ❹.

❾ ★★★ Tilikum Crossing Bridge.
If you return west on Division Street, between SE 8th and SE 9th avenues across the train tracks, you'll come to SE Tilikum Way, leading to the new Tilikum Crossing Bridge, opened in 2015. It's the country's longest bridge dedicated exclusively to bikes, pedestrians, and public transportation (i.e., no cars allowed) and offers a great connection between the Central Eastside and OMSI over to the new high-rise South Waterfront District on the west side, with great city views along the way. South Waterfront OHSU Commons (west side) or SE Division St. (east side).

Under the Tilikum Crossing bridge, follow the Eastbank Esplanade upriver to the Moda Center arena, where N. Interstate Avenue and then N. Williams Avenue take you to reach ❿ **Hopworks BikeBar,** the cycle-themed brewpub decorated with bike frames. Enjoy a giant pretzel and a pint from Hopworks Urban Brewery on the back patio—you earned it. 3947 N. Williams St. at Failing St. ☎ 503/237-6258. www.hopworksbeer.com. $.

⓫ ★★ Steel Bridge.
Return to the Eastbank Esplanade and complete your tour by crossing over the most eye-catching of Portland's bike-friendly bridges. Riders and pedestrians take a 220-foot cantilevered walkway suspended over the river, added on the south side in 2001. See p 18, ❼. ●

Dining Best Bets

Best **New** Restaurant
★★★ Alto Bajo $$
310 SW Stark St. (p 100)

Best for **Festive Celebrations**
★★★ Andina $$$
1314 NW Glisan St. (p 100)

Best for **Romance**
★ Chameleon $$$
2000 NE 40th Ave. (p 103)

Best for **Sophisticated Dining**
★★★ Blue Hour $$$
250 NW 13th Ave. (p 102)

Best **Dinner Entertainment**
★ Marrakesh $$
1201 NW 21st Ave. (p 105)

Best for **Gourmet Carnivores**
★★ Beast $$$
5425 NE 30th Ave. (p 101)

Best for **Vegetarians**
★ Prasad $ *925 NW Davis St. (p 108)*

Best **Italian**
★★ Caffè Mingo $$
807 NW 21st Ave. (p 102)

Best **Pan Asian**
★★ Pok Pok $$
3226 SE Division St. (p 107)

Best **Tapas**
★★★ Toro Bravo $$
120 NE Russell St. (p 111)

Best **Burger**
★★ Yakuza Lounge $$
5411 NE 30th Ave. (p 112)

Best **Pizza**
★ Apizza Scholls $$ *4741 SE Hawthorne Blvd. (p 100)*; and
★ Ken's Artisan Pizza $$ *304 SE 28th Ave. (p 104)*

Best for **Deli Delights**
★ Kenny & Zuke's Delicatessen $$
1038 SW Stark St. (p 104)

Best **Cheap Eats**
★ Bunk Sandwiches $
621 SE Morrison St. (p 102)

Best **Brunch**
★★ Tasty n Alder $$
580 SW 12th Ave. (p 111)

Best **Happy Hour**
★ Saucebox $$
214 SW Broadway Ave. (p 109)

Best **Desserts**
★★ Pazzo $$$
627 SW Washington St. (p 107)

Menu shopping outside Ava Gene's.
Previous page: Dessert at Paley's Place.

Downtown, Pearl & NW Dining

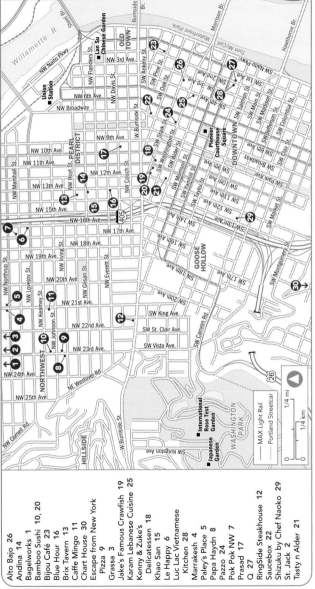

Southeast Dining

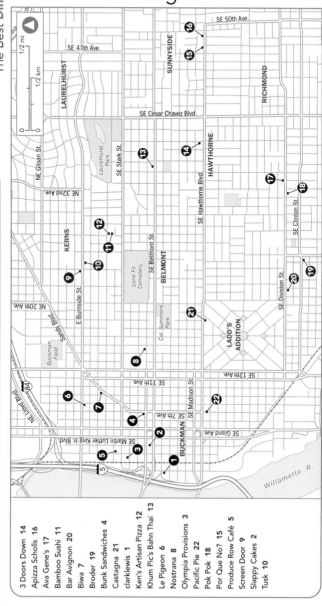

3 Doors Down **14**
Apizza Scholls **17**
Ava Gene's **17**
Bamboo Sushi **11**
Bar Avignon **20**
Biwa **7**
Broder **19**
Bunk Sandwiches **4**
Castagna **21**
clarklewis **1**
Ken's Artisan Pizza **12**
Khum Pic's Bahn Thai **13**
Le Pigeon **6**
Nostrana **8**
Olympia Provisions **3**
Pacific Pie **22**
Pok Pok **18**
Por Que No? **15**
Produce Row Café **5**
Screen Door **9**
Slappy Cakes **2**
Tusk **10**

North & Northeast Dining

Back to Eden Bakery
Café and Dessert Shop 7
Bamboo Sushi 6
Beast 9
Chameleon 13
Pambiche 11
Podnah's Pit 8
Pok Pok Noi 3

Shandong
Restaurant 12
Swiss Hibiscus 5
Tasty n Sons 2
Tin Shed 4
Toro Bravo 1
Yakuza Lounge 10

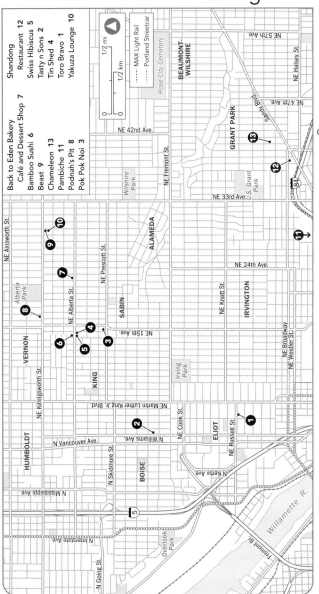

Dining A to Z

★★ 3 Doors Down HAW-THORNE *AMERICAN* This neighborhood cafe is a local darling for its happy hour with small-plate and drink specials, its dinner menu of inspired comfort food, its attentive service, and overall bang for the buck. *1429 SE 37th Ave. (at Hawthorne Blvd.).* ☎ *503/236-6886. www.3doorsdowncafe.com. Entrees $18–$25. Dinner Tues–Sun. Bus: 14. Map p 98.*

★★★ Alto Bajo DOWNTOWN MODERN MEXICAN The earthy flavors of Mexican cuisine are elevated to a higher plane at this sophisticated yet unpretentious place that opened in 2017. Fresh local fish, meat, and produce are combined to create dishes that are sometimes surprising in their richness and variety. The moles are really special. *310 SW Stark St. (in Hi-Lo hotel).* ☎ *971/222-2211. www.altobajopdx.com. Entrees $12–$30. All meals daily. MAX: SW 2nd & Oak. Map p 97.*

★★★ Andina PEARL *PERUVIAN* You've never had *nuevo andino*

cuisine like this: stuffed piquillo peppers, house-made ceviche, squash stew, and a huge variety of meat and fish dishes. Many plates are sized to share. Loud, lively atmosphere and very popular, so reserve well in advance. This has been one of Portland's top destination restaurants since 2003. *1314 NW Glisan St. (at 13th Ave.).* ☎ *503/228-9535. www.andinarestaurant.com. Entrees lunch $12–$18; dinner $18–$35. Lunch & dinner daily. Bus: 17. Map p 97.*

★ Apizza Scholls HAWTHORNE *PIZZA* Get in line early for some of Portland's best pizza—think hot truffle oil, goat horn peppers, and cured pork shoulder—and hope they don't run out of homemade dough, which does happen. Better yet, reserve a table and enjoy an antipasto before your pie. *4741 SE Hawthorne Blvd. (at 48th Ave.).* ☎ *503/233-1286. www.apizzascholls.com. Pizzas $19–$25. Dinner daily; lunch Sat–Sun. Bus: 14. Map p 98.*

★★★ Ava Gene's SE DIVISION *ITALIAN* I have never had a less

Andina's sophisticated twist on Peruvian food.

Bar Avignon.

than wonderful meal at this contemporary trattoria. The sophisticated, Italian-inspired cooking is inventive without being overly complicated. The ingredients are extremely fresh from the Pacific Northwest. Share some smaller plates and split a pasta dish and you'll leave happy. *3377 SE Division.* ☎ *971/229-0571. www.avagenes. com. Entrees $18–$37. Dinner daily. Bus: 4. Map p 98.*

★ **Back to Eden Bakery Café and Dessert Shop** ALBERTA *BAKERY* This eco-conscious concern, a café on one side with a dessert shop next door, is your source for gluten-free vegan meals, cookies, cakes, pies, and other goodies using mostly local, organic ingredients. *2217 NE Alberta St. (at 23rd Ave.).* ☎ *503/477-5022. www.back toedenbakery.com. Entrees $7–$13; desserts $3–$8. All meals daily. Bus: 72. Map p 99.*

★★ **kids Bagelworks** NORTHWEST *BAGELS* Sometimes nothing will do but a toasted bagel with lox and cream cheese. That's when you head to Bagelworks, the bagel-centric sister of Kenny & Zuke's Delicatessen (p 104). Order a breakfast bagel sandwich or a big pastrami, turkey, or whitefish-filled bagel for lunch. *2376 NW Thurman St.* ☎ *503/954-1737. www.kennyand zukes.com/bagelworks. Entrees*

$7.50–$15. Breakfast & lunch daily. Bus: 15. Map p 97.

★★★ **Bamboo Sushi** DOWNTOWN *SUSHI* The country's first certified sustainable sushi restaurant serves guilt-free seafood that happens to be delicious and beautifully plated. Other locations: 836 NW 23rd Ave. (☎ 971/229-1925); 1409 NE Alberta St. (☎ 503/889-0336); 310 SE 28th Ave. (☎ 503/232-5255). *404 SW 12th Ave.* ☎ *503/232-5335. www.bamboo sushi.com. Entrees $11–$35. Lunch & dinner daily. Streetcar: SW 12th & Couch. Bus: 20. Map p 97.*

★★ **Bar Avignon** CLINTON *PACIFIC NORTHWEST/FRENCH* Criminally delicious craft cocktails taste even better with foraged lettuces, homemade charcuterie, and artisan cheeses. Daily specials may range from rabbit agnolotti to halibut with onions. *2138 SE Division.* ☎ *503/517-0808. www.baravignon. com. Entrees $22–$27. Dinner daily. Bus: 4. Map p 98.*

★★ **Beast** ALBERTA *FRENCH/ AMERICAN* Local celeb chef Naomi Pomeroy's prix-fixe meat-centric meals—six-course seasonally changing dinners and a four-course brunch, all served at a communal table—will make carnivores swoon. *5425 NE 30th Ave. (at Killingsworth St.).* ☎ *503/841-6968.*

www.beastpdx.com. Dinner Wed–Sat $125; Sun brunch $40. Bus: 72. Map p 99.

★ **Bijou Café** DOWNTOWN AMERICAN Long before Portland had a food scene, Bijou was serving breakfast and lunch to happy downtown diners. It's the only place I know of that serves oyster hash. The popular Friday-night-only dinners feature live jazz. *132 SW Third Ave. ☎ 503/222-3187. www. bijoucafepdx.com. Entrees $7–$15. Breakfast & lunch daily; dinner Fri. MAX: Oak St. Map p 97.*

★ **Biwa** INNER SOUTHEAST JAPANESE Come downstairs into this cozy space for Japanese comfort/bar food like ramen bowls, grilled rice balls, and pickled everything, plus sushi, sashimi, and loads of sake choices. *215 SE 9th St. (at Ash St.). ☎ 503/239-8830. www. biwarestaurant.com. Entrees $6–$14. Lunch & dinner daily. Bus: 12, 19, 20, or 70. Map p 98.*

★★ **Blue Hour** PEARL MEDITERRANEAN/NEW AMERICAN This long-established restaurant helped put Portland on the foodie map. The menu offers just a few choices (fish, chicken, pork, steaks, pasta), always simply prepared and beautifully served. Expect only the freshest local ingredients and a superb wine list. This is a happy-hour hotspot for downtown and Pearl District professionals. Live jazz on Saturday nights. *250 NW 13th St. (at Everett). ☎ 503/226-3394. www.bluehouronline.com. Entrees $19–$44. Dinner daily; brunch Sat–Sun. Bus: 17. Map p 97.*

★ **Brix Tavern** PEARL AMERICAN This comfortable pub offers unpretentious but solid choices like wild-mushroom pizza, mac and cheese, and potpies, plus pool tables and sports on big screens. *1338 NW Hoyt St. (at 14th Ave.).*

☎ 503/943-5995. www.brixtavern. com. Entrees $10–$24. Lunch & dinner Mon–Fri; brunch & dinner Sat & Sun. Bus: 17. Map p 97.

★★ **Broder** CLINTON SWEDISH *Smaklig måltid!* Tuck into Danish pancakes, a Stockholm hot dog, and, of course, Swedish meatballs at this ever-popular Scandinavian eatery. Their box lunch is a winner. **Broder Nord,** 2508 N. Interstate Ave. (☎ 503/282-5555) serves a smorgasbord dinner on Fridays. *2508 SE Clinton St. (at 25th Ave.). ☎ 503/736-3333. www.broderpdx. com. Entrees $7–$16. Breakfast & lunch daily. Bus: 10. Map p 98.*

★ **Bunk Sandwiches** INNER SOUTHEAST SANDWICHES When you're hankering for a good breakfast or lunch sandwich, check out this unprepossessing spot serving a delectable pork belly *Cubano* and roast chicken salad with apple-wood smoked bacon and avocado. Consult the website for additional locations. *621 SE Morrison St. (at 6th Ave.). ☎ 503/477-9515. www.bunk sandwiches.com. Entrees $5–$12. Breakfast & lunch daily. Bus: 6 or 15. Map p 98.*

★★ **Caffè Mingo** NORTHWEST ITALIAN If you're looking for a friendly neighborhood restaurant serving fine, simple Italian food made with exclusively local ingredients, show up at Mingo. But show up early or late, or you'll have to wait—they don't take reservations. *807 NW 21st Ave. ☎ 503/226-4646. www.caffemingo.com. Entrees $13–$28. Lunch Tues–Fri; dinner Tues–Sun. Streetcar: NW 21st & Northrup. Map p 97.*

★★ **Castagna** HAWTHORNE MODERN EUROPEAN A prix-fixe dinner here is always a culinary adventure, with fresh ingredients and a mix of textures and flavors. Cafe Castagna next door is far less expensive with simpler Italian-inspired fare. *1752 SE Hawthorne Blvd. (at 17th Ave.).* ☎ 503/231-7373. www.castagnarestaurant.com. *Restaurant prix-fixe dinner $100; chef's tasting menu $165; cafe entrees $13–$28. Dinner Tues–Sun. Bus: 14. Map p 98.*

★★ **Chameleon** HOLLYWOOD *AMERICAN* This under-the-radar spot earns raves for its intimate atmosphere and covered patio as well as its array of mostly vegetarian and gluten-free small plates. Entrees are limited to about 5 choices, including duck breast and rack of lamb. Most of the produce comes from the chef's own farm. *2000 NE 40th Ave. (at U.S. Grant Place).* ☎ 503/460-2682. www.chameleonpdx.com. *Entrees $26–$38; small plates $9–$14. Dinner Wed–Sat. Bus: 75. Map p 99.*

★ **Chart House** SOUTHWEST *SEAFOOD/AMERICAN* Portlanders have patronized this restaurant for decades because it has one of the best views in the city. Foodies tend to ignore it because it's part of a chain and, though fresh and well-prepared, there's nothing cutting-edge about its traditionally prepared dishes. But for reliably good food with a view, you can count on Chart House. Also good for happy hour and weekend brunch. *5700 SW Terwilliger Blvd.* ☎ 503/246-6963. www.chart-house.com. *Entrees lunch $12–$27; dinner $26–$42. Lunch Mon–Fri; dinner daily; brunch Sun. Bus: 1. Map p 97.*

★★ **clarklewis** INNER SOUTHEAST *AMERICAN* Sliding garage doors and a fireplace give one of Portland's original farm-to-table restaurants a cozy "industrial chic" atmosphere, with an open kitchen turning out savory dishes such as grilled lamb and black cod, plus pastas and farm-fresh vegetable accompaniments. *1001 SE Water Ave. #160 (at Yamhill St.).* ☎ 503/235-2294. www.clarklewispdx.com. *Entrees $15–$35. Lunch Mon–Fri; dinner daily. Bus: 15. Map p 98.*

★ **Escape from New York Pizza** NORTHWEST *PIZZA* When you want to escape from all that is trendy in Portland, order a slice or a pie-to-go at this funky hole-in-the-wall founded in 1983. There are usually two of three simple pies available by the slice, maybe sausage, maybe pepperoni, maybe veggie, maybe mushroom and olive. The price is low and the only other thing they sell is a Caesar salad. *622 NW 23rd Ave.* ☎ 503/227-5243. www.efnypizza.net. *Slice $4–$4.50. Lunch & dinner daily. Bus: 15. Map p 97.*

★★ **Grassa** NORTHWEST *ITALIAN* This trattoria-type spot on NW 23rd offers made-on-the-premises pasta augmented with seasonally

Farm-to-table cuisine at clarklewis.

changing sauces. About seven pasta dishes are offered daily, including spaghetti *agli'olio* (with olive oil), spaghetti *pomodoro* (with tomato sauce), and spaghetti lemon *chitarra* made with basil and hazelnuts and topped with zucchini and mozzarella crema. Order a salad or a starter plate of fried zucchini fritters to accompany your pasta and you've got a top-notch lunch or dinner for under $20. *1506 NW 23rd Ave.* ☎ *917/386-2196. www.grassapdx.com. Entrees $11– $15. Lunch & dinner daily. Streetcar: NW 23rd & Marshall. Map p 97.*

★ Jake's Famous Crawfish

DOWNTOWN *SEAFOOD* Portland's oldest restaurant, this atmospheric warren of rooms features an ornate bar and a menu dedicated to fish and meat cooked in fairly traditional ways. Jake's is famous for its crawfish, which come from Lake Billy Chinook in Oregon's high desert; they're available from May through October and made into a spicy Cajun-style stew. Expensive, but come for lunch of at happy hour and you can enjoy less expensive small plates. *401 SW 12th Ave. (at Stark St.).* ☎ *503/226-1419. www. jakesfamouscrawfish.com. Lunch $12–$19; dinner $20–$47. Lunch & dinner Mon–Sat; dinner Sun. Streetcar: SW 10th & Stark. Map p 97.*

★★ Karam Lebanese Cuisine

DOWNTOWN *LEBANESE/SYRIAN* Friendly service and consistently good Lebanese dishes like couscous, kebobs, hummus, stuffed grape leaves, vegetable mezzes and fresh-baked pita bread set this place apart. It's a popular downtown lunch spot. *515 SW 4th Ave.* ☎ *503/223-0830. www.karam restaurant.com. Lunch $6.50–$11; dinner $14–$24. Lunch & dinner daily. Bus: 15 or 51. Map p 97.*

★ Kenny & Zuke's Delicatessen

DOWNTOWN *DELI* This is Portland, so it's not just deli food, it's *artisan-made* deli food. All your faves are here: chicken soup with matzoh balls, chopped liver, latkes, blintzes, knishes, and overstuffed hot pastrami sandwiches. *1038 SW Stark St. (at 11th Ave.).* ☎ *503/222-3354. www.kennyandzukes.com. Entrees $10–$18. All meals daily. Streetcar: SW 10th & Stark. Map p 97.*

★★ Ken's Artisan Pizza

SOUTHEAST *PIZZA* With an emphasis on the "art," the crisp-crusted pies at this stone-oven pizzeria are worth the wait. Try the prosciutto and *soppressata. 304 SE 28th Ave. (at Pine St.).* ☎ *503/517-9951.www.kensartisan.com. Entrees $12–$17. Dinner daily. Bus: 28. Map p 98.*

Happiness Is a Portland Happy Hour

Happy hour has become a big thing in Portland, but not just because you can get a great cocktail or glass of wine or beer at a reduced price. It's the food that goes with the beverages that draws those after-work crowds. Check out the websites of just about every restaurant listed here and you'll find times listed for happy hour (generally btw. 4 and 6pm). It's a great way to sample some of the restaurant's best dishes, served as small plates, at about half the cost.

★ **Khao San** PEARL DISTRICT *THAI* Food cart turned restaurant, this simple and inexpensive Pearl District eatery serves consistently good Thai food, but be aware of your spice-tolerance or your meal may blow the top of your head off. I like the pad Thai noodles and the spring rolls. *1435 NW Flanders. (at 14th Ave.).* ☎ *503/227-3700. www. khaosanpdx.com. Entrees $12–$16. Lunch & dinner daily. Streetcar: NW 11th & Glisan. Map p 97.*

★ **Khun Pic's Bahn Thai** BEL-MONT *THAI* It looks like someone's old Victorian house, but it's actually one of Portland's most authentic Thai eateries, albeit with leisurely service. And I mean that. There is one cook and one server and if you're in a hurry, dine elsewhere. If you enjoy unique dining experiences, you'll enjoy the home-cooked dishes and sauces served in this meticulously restored house. *3429 SE Belmont St. (at 34th Ave.).* ☎ *503/235-1610. Entrees $8–$14. No credit cards. Dinner Wed–Sat. Bus: 15. Map p 98.*

★ **Le Happy** NORTHWEST *CRE-PERIE* Sweet and savory crepes are served in a charming red-walled nook. The crepe fillings are classic combinations with cheese, ham, salmon, and other goodies, and you can add half a steak and a salad for $9. *1011 NW 16th Ave. (at Lovejoy St.).* ☎ *503/226-1258. www.lehappy. com. Entrees $8–$15. Dinner Mon–Sat; brunch Sat–Sun. Streetcar: NW Marshall & 18th; Bus: 77. Map p 97.*

★★★ **Le Pigeon** INNER SOUTH-EAST *FRENCH* An open kitchen and a James Beard Award–winning chef (Gabriel Rucker) make this snug spot a consistent standout. It's a creative spin on traditional French cuisine, from grilled pigeon to beef cheek bourguignon and ricotta-parmesan dumplings. Make a reservation now and you might get in. *738 E Burnside St. (at 7th Ave.).* ☎ *503/546-8796. www.le pigeon.com. Entrees $17–$39. Dinner daily. Bus: 12, 19, or 20. Map p 98.*

★ **Luc Lac Vietnamese Kitchen** DOWNTOWN *VIETNAMESE* It's loud, fun, and serves good food, but if you hate standing in line (no reservations accepted), better come early or late. Pho is a favorite dish here and comes with beef, chicken, or tofu or veggies for a slurpy, satisfying meal. Vegetarians have many choices, including a peanut curry with tofu. On Fridays and Saturdays, Luc Lac stays open until 4am and becomes a kind of club-with-food scene. *835 SW 2nd Ave. (at Taylor St.).* ☎ *503/222-0047. www.luclackitchen.com. Entrees $9–$12. Lunch & dinner daily. MAX: SW Madison and 1st. Map p 97.*

★ **Marrakesh** NORTHWEST *MOROCCAN* Come for the surprisingly good Moroccan specialties served in an exotic North African environment and enjoy belly dancing as you sip your fragrant mint tea. There's a special five-course fixed-price dinner available for groups of 4 or more. *1201 NW 21st Ave. (at 22nd St.).* ☎ *503/248-9442. www.marrakeshportland.com.*

The open kitchen at Le Pigeon.

The bar at Olympia Provisions.

Entrees $13–$24, 5-course dinner $24. Dinner daily. Streetcar: NW Marshall & 22nd. Bus: 77. Map p 97.

★★ **Nostrana** INNER SOUTHEAST *ITALIAN* The wood-oven pizzas and pasta dishes get high praise, but it's the little details that help make Nostrana special, like the fresh-crushed olive oil for dipping your home-baked bread. Cathy Whims is a champion of simple Italian cooking using the freshest of local ingredients. Good for lunch, too, with great pork sandwiches. *1401 SE Morrison St. (at 14th Ave.).* ☎ *503/234-2427. www. nostrana.com. Lunch $10–$19; dinner $19–29. Lunch Mon–Fri; dinner daily. Bus: 15. Map p 98.*

★★ **Olympia Provisions** INNER SOUTHEAST *CHARCUTERIE* The big lighted sign that says "MEAT" sums up this place, which offers the best salami, sausage, bratwurst, franks, and charcuterie plates in town. All the products are handcrafted. This ain't your typical hot dog vendor! There's a second location at 1384 SE Division St. (☎ 503/ 384-2259). *126 SW 2nd Ave. (in Pine St. Market).* ☎ *917/386-2199. www. olympiaprovisions.com. Entrees $14– $18. Lunch & dinner daily. MAX: SW 3rd & Oak. Map p 98.*

★ **Pacific Pie** EASTSIDE INDUSTRIAL *BRITISH* Here you'll find those savory meat pies the Brits invented and that don't often appear on American menus:

shepherd's pie, lamb pie, steak pie, pork pie, fish pie—and the more familiar chicken pot pie. The ingredients are fresh and local, and entrees come with soup or salad. Gluten-free and vegetarian casseroles, wraps, and pies are also available. Oh yes, the sweet kind of pie is available, too, and just as good. *1520 SE 7th Ave.* ☎ *503/381-6157. www.pacificpie.com. Entrees $13– $15. Lunch & dinner daily. Streetcar: SE Grand & Main. Map p 98.*

★★ **Paley's Place** NORTHWEST *FRENCH* Iron Chef America and James Beard award winner Vitaly Paley helped to start the Portland food craze back in 1995 in this Victorian home in Nob Hill. The menu relies on locally sourced meat and produce, with dishes such as marinated and grilled quail, and butternut squash and goat cheese ravioli. *204 NW 21st Ave. (at Northrup St.).* ☎ *503/243-2403. www.paleysplace. net. Entrees $17–$36. Dinner daily. Streetcar: NW Marshall & 22nd. Bus: 17. Map p 97.*

★ **Pambiche** NORTHEAST *CUBAN* You can't miss the colorful building, and the Cuban creole food is just as exciting, from the "Plato Comunista" (beans and rice) to the classic rubbed pork sandwiches and braised oxtails. *2811 NE Glisan St. (at 28th Ave.).* ☎ *503/233-0511. Entrees $9–$17. Lunch & dinner daily; brunch Sat–Sun. Bus: 19. Map p 99.*

★ **Papa Haydn** NORTHWEST *AMERICAN* The food at this long-established restaurant is reliably good if not adventurous, but that's also what the patrons like. Nice spot to lunch on "Trendy-third." *701 NW 23rd Ave. (at Irving St.).* ☎ *503/228-7317. www.papahaydn. com. Entrees $13–$26. Lunch & dinner daily. Bus: 15. Map p 97.*

★★ **Pazzo** DOWNTOWN *ITALIAN/PACIFIC NORTHWEST* This time-honored downtown restaurant excels with its homemade pastas. The pappardelle "with grandma's special Sunday meat sauce" (a veal, pork, and beef ragu) is meraviglioso, and the Caesar salad is maybe the best in town. Inspired desserts, too, but those are not necessarily Italian. *627 SW Washington St. (in Hotel Vintage).* ☎ *503/228-1515. www.pazzo.com. Entrees $19–$36. All meals daily. MAX: Pioneer Sq. Map p 97.*

★ **Podnah's Pit** NORTHEAST *BBQ* The place to go for Southern BBQ done right. Plates of pulled pork, ribs, chicken, brisket, sausage, and trout come with cornbread and two sides (go for the potato salad and collard greens). You can also get a saucy pulled pork or brisket sandwich. *1625 NE Killingsworth St. (at 17th Ave.).* ☎ *503/281-3700. www.podnahspit.com. Entrees $13–$17. Lunch & dinner daily; brunch Sat–Sun. Bus: 8. Map p 99.*

★★★ **Pok Pok** SOUTHEAST *ASIAN* You may not be able to pronounce the names of the dishes, but you'll sure be able to taste them. A pioneer in the Portland food scene, Pok Pok's tasty take on Asian street food makes it a local favorite. Their Vietnamese fish-sauce wings are a Portland classic. Come early or late or you'll have to wait because they don't take reservations and the place is always hopping. It's so popular that Pok Pok has now expanded locally (and nationally). At **Pok Pok NW** (1639 NW Marshall St.; ☎ **971/351-1946**), you can reserve a table; at **Pok Pok Noi** (1469 NE Prescott; ☎ 503/287-4149), you can't. *3226 SE Division St. (at 32nd Ave.).* ☎ *503/232-1387. www.pokpokpdx. com. Entrees $9–$14. Daily lunch & dinner. Bus: 4. Map p 97.*

Local favorite Pok Pok serves tasty Asian dishes.

Casual Prassad specializes in organic, vegan food.

★ **Por Que No?** HAWTHORNE *MEXICAN* "Why not?" indeed— this colorful *taqueria* is *excelente* in the atmosphere and food departments both, especially during sidewalk-dining weather. There's a large and reasonably priced taco, tamale, and quesadilla menu. *4635 SE Hawthorne Blvd. (at 46th St.).* ☎ *503/954-3138. www.porqueno tacos.com. Tacos $3.50–$5; entrees $7–$12. Daily lunch & dinner. Bus: 14. Map p 98.*

★ **Prasad** PEARL *VEGETARIAN* The name means "holy food" in Sanskrit, and the menu is all organic, gluten-free, and vegan. Choices include curry bowls, wraps, salads, and tempeh scrambles. Located in Yoga Pearl, so you can do your sun salutes before or after dining. *925 NW Davis St. (at 9th Ave.).* ☎ *503/224-3993. www.prasad cuisine.com. Entrees $9–$9. All meals daily. Streetcar: NW 10th & Everett. Map p 97.*

Gourmet pub fare at Produce Row Cafe.

★ **Produce Row Café** INNER
SOUTHEAST *AMERICAN* Gourmet
pub fare—cheese steaks, meatloaf,
a stellar burger—and an outdoor
patio put this Inner Southeast destination on the map. All kinds of
fresh, interesting versions of comfort food for all dietary preferences.
204 SE Oak St. (at 2nd Ave.).
☎ *503/232-8355. www.produce
rowcafe.com. Entrees $9–$22. Lunch
& dinner daily. Bus: 6. Map p 98.*

★★ **Q** DOWNTOWN *PACIFIC
NORTHWEST* After a 50-year run
as the Veritable Quandary, this
ever-popular restaurant moved to a
new location, changed its name,
and rethought some of its menu.
The cooking is always good and
the atmosphere is undeniably cozy.
Try the beef stroganoff or white
bean soup with collard greens and
ham. Heck, try anything, it's all
super-fresh and locally sourced. *828
SW 2nd Ave. (at Taylor St.).*
☎ *503/850-8195. www.q-portland.
com. Entrees $13–$$31. Lunch Mon–
Fri; dinner daily; brunch Sat–Sun.
MAX: Morrison SW 3rd. Map p 97.*

★★ **RingSide Steakhouse**
NORTHWEST *STEAKHOUSE*
Food the way it used to be in the
old-fashioned days before the revolution. Dining at Stumptown's oldest steakhouse isn't cheap, but the
steaks are super, there's an outstanding wine list, and the onion
rings were praised by James Beard
himself. That's why this place has
been popular for 70 years and is
still going strong. *2165 W. Burnside
St. (at King Ave.).* ☎ *503/223-1513.
www.ringsidesteakhouse.com.
Entrees $23–$55. Dinner daily. Bus:
15, 18, or 20. Map p 97.*

★ **Saucebox** DOWNTOWN *PAN-
ASIAN* A youngish crowd sips creative cocktails and nibbles dim
sum, ramen, and curries as DJs spin
in the evenings; earlier, smart

singles come for the super happy
hour deals. Everyone loves the soft-
shell crab buns. *214 SW Broadway
(at Pine St.).* ☎ *503/241-3393. www.
saucebox.com. Entrees $9–$28. Dinner Tues–Sat. Bus: 1, 12, 19, 20, 54,
or 56. Map p 97.*

★ **Screen Door** SOUTHEAST
SOUTHERN Here you'll find favorites from across the South, including shrimp and grits, beef brisket,
and their celebrated buttermilk-
battered fried chicken. Or how
about praline bacon as a starter, or
glazed hushpuppies for breakfast?
There's a reason why there's always
a line for the weekend brunch. *2337
E. Burnside St. (at 24th Ave.).*
☎ *503/542-0880. www.screendoor
restaurant.com. Entrees $10–$18. All
meals daily. Bus: 20. Map p 98.*

★ **Shandong Restaurant**
NORTHEAST *CHINESE* A bright
spot in Portland's subpar Chinese-
food scene, Shandong offers reasonably priced dishes from
northern China, such as crab curry
and cherry pork, plus house-made
noodles. *3724 NE Broadway St. (at
37th Ave.).* ☎ *503/287-0331. www.
shandongportland.com. Entrees
$8–$15. Lunch & dinner daily. Bus:
77. Map p 99.*

★★ **Shizuku by Chef Naoko**
DOWNTOWN *JAPANESE* After
years of being a bento lunch spot,
Chef Naoko reopened as Shizuku, a
dinner-only restaurant with a spare,
elegant interior designed by famed
Japanese architect Kengo Kuma.
The emphasis is on seasonal
organic local ingredients with Japanese fish and seafood not otherwise available in Oregon. *1237 SW
Jefferson St. (at 12th Ave.).* ☎ *503/
227-4136. www.chefnaoko.com.
Entrees $8–$19. Lunch Tues–Sat; dinner Wed–Fri. Bus: 6, 43, 45, 55, 58,
or 68. Map p 97.*

Pod People

In recent years, food carts have become an essential part of the Portland "brand." These mobile food purveyors merge the city's idiosyncratic, do-it-yourself character with its local passion for good food at a good price. The carts park in clusters (or "pods") in different neighborhoods all over the city Here are some of the more established spots:

Downtown:
- SW 5th Avenue and Oak Street (the original Portland pod)
- SW 9th and 10th avenues between Alder and Washington streets

North & Northeast:
- N Mississippi Street and Skidmore Avenue (Mississippi Marketplace)
- NE 21st Avenue and Alberta Street

Southeast:
- SE 12th Avenue and Hawthorne Boulevard (Cartopia)
- SE 32nd Avenue and Division Street (D Street Noshery)
- SE 43rd Avenue and Belmont Street (Good Food Here)
- SE 50th Avenue and Ivon Street (A La Carts)

For other locations and cartloads of information on Portland food carts, go to www.foodcartsportland.com. At this site, you can book a **food-cart tour.** The walking tours are offered Monday through Friday starting around noon at a downtown food cart and last for 60-90 minutes. The $50 tour price includes small bites at four different food carts in different locations. The 3-hour Food Cart Tour offered by **Pedal Bike Tours** (133 SW Second Ave. (www.pedalbiketours. com; ☎ **503/243-2453**), visits favorite food carts in different neighborhoods for $69 (the price includes samples at all the carts).

★ **Slappy Cakes** BELMONT
AMERICAN A restaurant where you make your own pancakes? Yup, and it's both fun, flavorful, and family-friendly. You order a portion of batter, make your pancakes at the table, and then add all the sweet or savory toppings you want. If you don't want to do your own cooking in a restaurant, you can order breakfast dishes prepared in the kitchen. Your kids will love their interactive meal and it's a good place to fool your date into thinking that you know how to cook. *246 SE Belmont.*

☎ *503/477-4805. www.slappycakes. com. Pancake batter $7, topping $2.50; entrees $10–$14. Breakfast & lunch daily. Bus: 15. Map p 98.*

★★ **St. Jack** NORTHWEST
FRENCH Many of the dishes here are old-school French cafe classics, with tastes that are delightfully worth rediscovering. Try the cream of tomato soup cooked in a puff pastry, seared foie gras on brioche, or the Lyonnaise onion tart. Fish, mussels, and steak and frites are on the menu, too, of course. *1610 NW*

23rd Ave. ☎ 503/360-1281. www.
stjackpdx.com. Entrees $11–$37. Dinner daily. Bus: 15. Map p 99.

★ **Swiss Hibiscus** ALBERTA
SWISS Swiss cuisine with a Hawaiian influence (seriously), from fondue
to Wiener schnitzel, bratwurst and
goulash, draws fans to this hidden
gem—as does the famous house-
made salad dressing. *4950 NW 14th
Ave. (at Alberta St.).* ☎ 503/477-
9224. www.martinsswissdressing.
com. Entrees $12–$17. Lunch Wed;
dinner Tues–Sat. Bus: 72. Map p 99.

★★ **Tasty n Alder** DOWNTOWN
PACIFIC NORTHWEST Bustling,
unpretentious, and on everyone's
short list, this downtown restaurant—
sister to Toro Bravo (below) and
Tasty n Sons (below)—is a shared-
plate kind of place with dishes like
crispy fried oysters, radicchio salad,
and alder-plank-baked salmon.
Super-popular for weekend brunch.
580 SW 12th Ave. (at Alder St.).

Spanish tapas rule at Toro Bravo.

☎ 503/621-9251. www.tastynalder.
com. Entrees $15–$44. All meals
daily. Streetcar: SW 11th & Alder.
Map p 97.

★★ **Tasty n Sons** NORTH PORT-
LAND *AMERICAN* Bacon-wrapped
dates with maple syrup are just the
beginning at this sister restaurant
to Toro Bravo (below) and Tasty n
Alder (above). The menu here
tends towards Southern comfort,
with dishes like fried chicken and
BBQ ribs. Known for its gourmet
brunches, too, served daily until
2:30pm. *3808 N. Williams Ave. (at
Failing St.).* ☎ 503/621-1400. www.
tastynsons.com. Entrees $8–$24.
Brunch & dinner daily. Bus: 44. Map
p 99.

★ **Tin Shed** ALBERTA *AMERICAN*
Vying for the title of top breakfast
in town, this "garden cafe" also
does a solid lunch and dinner—but
starters like sweet-potato French
toast and biscuits with bacon gravy
are the real draw. Filling and
friendly with something for everyone, including the kids. *1438 NE
Alberta St. (at 14th Place).*
☎ 503/288-6966. www.tinshed
gardencafe.com. Entrees $7–$22. All
meals daily. Bus: 72. Map p 99.

★★★ **Toro Bravo** NORTHEAST
SPANISH There's a reason why this
Spanish tapas place is on everyone's
top five list: The food is remarkably
good and reasonably priced, and
the service is attitude-free. Eating
here means tapas time—share several plates to enjoy the full array of
tastes and textures. Highly recommended: salt cod fritters with aioli,
fried Spanish anchovies with fennel
and lemon, oxtail croquettes with
chili mayonnaise, and grilled aspar-
agus with fried ham. Expect a line.
120 NE Russell St. (at Rodney Ave.).
☎ 503/281-4464. www.torobravo
pdx.com. Tapas $3–$17. Dinner daily.
Bus: 6. Map p 99.

Portland Specialties

Regional Northwest cooking is distinguished by its pairings of meats and seafood with local greens, vegetables, fruits, and wines. Salmon (king, Coho, chinook) is the king of Oregon fish, though, to be honest, most of the salmon served and sold in Portland is now from Alaska. Salmon is prepared in seemingly endless ways, but the most traditional method is **alder-planked salmon.** This Native American cooking style entails preparing a salmon as a single filet, splaying it on alder wood, and slow-cooking it over a wood fire. After salmon, **Dungeness crab** is the region's top seafood offering, and crab cakes and crab salads are ubiquitous on Oregon restaurant menus during the crabbing season. The Northwest's combination of climate and abundant rainfall has also made Oregon one of the nation's major **fruit-growing regions,** producing a bounty of pears, blushing Rainier cherries, and berries, including strawberries, raspberries, and blackberries. **Wild mushrooms** are featured on menus throughout the city, so by all means try to have some while you're here. Oregon is also one of the few places in the world that still grows **hazelnuts.**

★★ **Tusk** SOUTHEAST *MIDDLE EASTERN/PACIFIC NORTHWEST* Tusk combines local ingredients with Middle Eastern spices and cooking techniques to create distinctive dishes that are rich in taste and texture. House-made chickpea fries, couscous and tagines, cooked-to-order flatbreads and skewers of hearth-roasted meats and fish are just some of the delights you'll find here. Lots of plant-centric dishes make this a hot spot for vegetarians. It's a scene place with lots of loud yakking so

be prepared. *2448 E. Burnside.* ☎ *503/894-8082. www.tuskpdx. com. Entrees $14–$32. Dinner daily; brunch Sat–Sun. Bus: 20. Map p 98.*

★★ **Yakuza Lounge** NORTHEAST *JAPANESE* Serving a contemporary version of Japanese bar food, this place offers many small plates to share and an outstanding burger (Kobe beef, of course). *5411 NE 30th Ave. (at Killingsworth St.).* ☎ *503/450-0893. www.yakuza-lounge.com. Entrees $10–$18. Dinner Wed–Sun. Bus: 72. Map p 99.* ●

Portland Nightlife

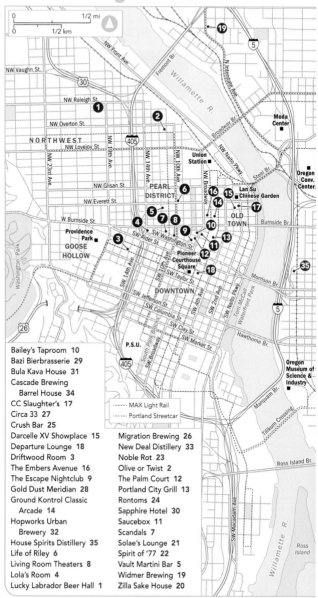

Bailey's Taproom 10
Bazi Bierbrasserie 29
Bula Kava House 31
Cascade Brewing
 Barrel House 34
CC Slaughter's 17
Circa 33 27
Crush Bar 25
Darcelle XV Showplace 15
Departure Lounge 18
Driftwood Room 3
The Embers Avenue 16
The Escape Nightclub 9
Gold Dust Meridian 28
Ground Kontrol Classic
 Arcade 14
Hopworks Urban
 Brewery 32
House Spirits Distillery 35
Life of Riley 6
Living Room Theaters 8
Lola's Room 4
Lucky Labrador Beer Hall 1

Migration Brewing 26
New Deal Distillery 33
Noble Rot 23
Olive or Twist 2
The Palm Court 12
Portland City Grill 13
Rontoms 24
Sapphire Hotel 30
Saucebox 11
Scandals 7
Solae's Lounge 21
Spirit of '77 22
Vault Martini Bar 5
Widmer Brewing 19
Zilla Sake House 20

······ MAX Light Rail
······ Portland Streetcar

Previous page: A flaming cocktail at the Driftwood Room.

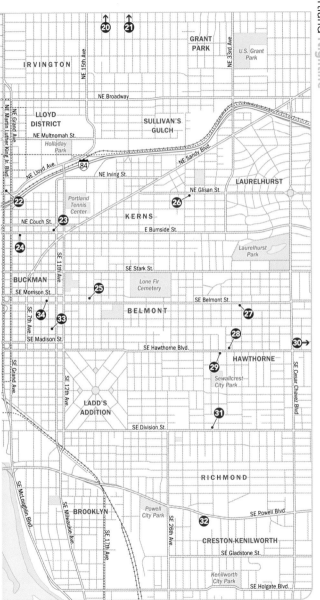

Nightlife Best Bets

Best View
★ Departure Lounge, *525 SW Morrison St. (p 117)*; and
★ Portland City Grill, *111 SW 5th Ave. #3000 (p 118)*

Best Live Jazz
★★ Solae's Lounge, *1801 NE Alberta St. (p 121)*

Best Place to Catch the Game
★ Spirit of '77, *500 NE Martin Luther King Jr. Blvd. (p 122)*

Best Dance Club Experience
★★ The Escape Nightclub, *333 SW Park Ave. (p 120)*

Best Sake Selection
★★ Zilla Sake House, *1806 NE Alberta St. (p 118)*

Best Martini
★★ Olive or Twist, *925 NW 11th Ave. (p 121)*

Best Draft Beer Selection
★★ Bailey's Taproom, *213 SW Broadway (p 117)*

Best Classy Watering Hole
★★ The Palm Court, *309 SW Broadway (p 117)*

Best for Romantic Snuggling
★★ Sapphire Hotel, *5008 SE Hawthorne Blvd. (p 118)*

Best Drag Show
★★ Darcelle XV Showplace, *208 NW 3rd Ave. (p 120)*

Best Gaming Experience
★★ Ground Kontrol Classic Arcade, *511 NW Couch St. (p 121)*

Best Authentic Old-Portland Brewpub
★ Widmer Brewing, *955 N. Russell St. (p 119)*

Best Retro Lounge
★★ Driftwood Room, *729 SW 15th Ave. (p 117)*

Best Alcohol Alternative
★ Bula Kava House, *3115 SE Division St. (p 121)*

Portland Nightlife A to Z

Early evening drinks at the rooftop Departure Lounge.

Bars & Lounges

★★ **Bailey's Taproom** DOWN-TOWN A great, wide-windowed location downtown and 20 constantly rotating taps (not to mention dozens of bottles) set this place apart from its competitors. *213 SW Broadway (at Ankeny St.).* ☎ 503/295-1004. www.baileystaproom.com. MAX: SW 6th & Pine St. Map p 114.

★ **Bazi Bierbrasserie** HAW-THORNE Like Belgian beer? Tripel, Abbey, Delirium Tremens—you name it, this place has it (over 20 on tap at last count), along with Euro-style pub food (Flemish frites!), and sidewalk seating. *1522 SE 32nd Ave. (at Hawthorne Blvd.).* ☎ 503/234-8888. www.bazipdx.com. Bus: 14. Map p 114.

★★ **Circa 33** BELMONT The drinks here focus on the classics—it's named after the year Prohibition was repealed—as well as the cutting edge, with an emphasis on whiskey. Check out the intimate alleyway seating. *3348 SE Belmont St. (at 34th Ave.).* ☎ 503/477-7682. www.circa33.com. Bus: 15. Map p 114.

★★ **Departure Lounge** DOWN-TOWN A little slice of L.A. overlooking downtown, this pop-chic rooftop lounge and Asian-fusion restaurant on top of the Nines hotel has pricey drinks, but the summer views are worth it. Nothing else like it in Portland. *525 SW Morrison St. (at 5th Ave.).* ☎ 503/802-5370. www.departureportland.com. MAX: Pioneer Courthouse/SW 6th Ave. Map p 114.

★★★ **Driftwood Room** DOWNTOWN Preserved from the 1950s, the Hotel deLuxe's dim little hideaway offers a great happy hour menu and specialty cocktails themed after the Golden Age of Hollywood. Try the violet-hued Elizabeth Taylor. *729 SW 15th Ave. (at Yamhill St.).* ☎ 503/219-2094. MAX: Providence Park. Map p 114.

★ **Gold Dust Meridian** HAW-THORNE Practically oozing illicit romance, this candlelit place serves scorpion bowls for sharing under a velvet painting of a nude, and boasts the longest happy hour in town (daily 2–8pm). *3267 SE Hawthorne Blvd. (at 32nd Ave.).* ☎ 503/239-1143. www.golddustmeridian.com. Bus: 14. Map p 114.

★★★ **The Palm Court** DOWN-TOWN Two words sum up the Benson Hotel's grand lobby bar: old school. Stiff bourbon drinks and delish happy hour bites make it a place your grandfather would love, too. Live jazz Wednesday to Saturday starting at 8:30pm. *309 SW Broadway (at Oak St.).* ☎ *503/228-2000. Bus: 1, 12, 16, 19, or 94. Map p 114.*

★★ **Portland City Grill** DOWNTOWN Arrive early for a window seat to catch the sunset from the 30th floor, and you just might stick around for dinner (steaks and seafood) or some late-evening jazz and flirting. *111 SW 5th Ave. #3000 (at Pine St.).* ☎ *503/450-0030. www. portlandcitygrill.com. MAX: SW 5th & Oak St. Map p 114.*

★ **Rontoms** INNER SOUTHEAST Too cool for a sign (look for the helicopter backpack logo), this mod lounge has a superb back patio with a fire pit and planters, and homemade ice cream on the menu. *600 E Burnside St. (at 6th Ave.).* ☎ *503/236-4536. www.rontoms.net. Bus: 12, 19, or 20. Map p 114.*

★★ **Sapphire Hotel** HAWTHORNE No longer the haunt of transient sailors and ladies of the night, this place preserves a maroon, candlelit version of its seamy past, now with food and outstanding cocktails. *5008 SE Hawthorne Blvd. (at 50th Ave.).* ☎ *503/232-6333. www.thesapphirehotel. com. Bus: 14. Map p 114.*

★★ **Saucebox** DOWNTOWN Nightly DJs transform the bar half of this pan-Asian restaurant into a dark, cacophonous dance club populated by Portland's stylish set. *214 SW Broadway (at Ankeny St.).* ☎ *503/241-3393. www.saucebox. com. MAX: SW 6th & Pine St. Map p 114.*

★★ **Zilla Sake House** ALBERTA *Kampai!* This sushi spot stocks dozens of kinds of sake—the largest selection west of the Mississippi, supposedly. They're happy to help you choose the right *junmai ginjo* to go with your dragon roll. *1806 NE Alberta St. (at 18th Ave.).* ☎ *503/288-8372. www.zillasake house.com. Bus: 72. Map p 114.*

Breweries & Brewpubs

★ **Cascade Brewing Barrel House** BELMONT Sour beers aged up to a year in wine, port, or whiskey oak barrels are the specialty of this Southeast brewpub—an acquired taste, for sure, but no one does them better. *939 SE Belmont St. (at 10th Ave.).* ☎ *503/265-8603. www.cascadebrewingbarrel house.com. Bus: 15. Map p 114.*

★★ **Hopworks Urban Brewery** SOUTHEAST Sustainability is a priority here, starting with the organic beers and food, and extending to the recycled materials

Sour beer tasting at Cascade Brewing Barrel House.

Hopworks serves craft beer in an industrial-chic setting.

used in the industrial-ski-lodge setting. Cyclists should steer to their **BikeBar** (3947 N. Williams Ave.; see p 94). *2944 SE Powell Blvd. (at 30th Ave.).* ☎ *503/232-4677. www.hopworksbeer.com. Bus: 9. Map p 114.*

★ Lucky Labrador Beer Hall

NORTHWEST Portland's version of a German *bierhaus* occupies a former trucking warehouse complete with a 5-ton crane in the rafters. Dogs and babies are welcome in this casual spot. *1945 NW Quimby St. (at 20th Ave.).* ☎ *503/517-4352. www.luckylab.com. Streetcar: NW Northrup & 18th. Bus: 77. Map p 114.*

★★ Migration Brewing

NORTHEAST The ultra-smooth cream ale on the nitro tap is dangerously good at this relaxed neighborhood brewery, with picnic tables outside and a dartboard inside. *2828 NE Glisan St. (at 29th Ave.).* ☎ *503/206-5221. www.migrationbrewing.com. Bus: 17. Map p 114.*

★★ Widmer Brewing ALBERTA

The city's largest craft brewer has run this pub in the semi-industrial zone near the river in North Portland since 1984. German food fills the menu, and free brewery tours run on Friday (3pm) and Saturday

Beer!

With more breweries than any other city on Earth and half a dozen annual beer-themed festivals, Portland lays strong claim to being the world's most brew-crazy (beeriest?) metropolis. Thank the profusion of local ingredients (especially Willamette Valley hops) and accommodating state laws—but it's mostly due to the sheer enthusiasm and innovation of local brewers, who turn out some of the best lagers, ales, porters, and stouts you'll find anywhere. You could arrange an entire visit just around the city's brewpubs, or take a guided tour of craft breweries aboard the **Brew Bus** ($45, www.brewbus.com) or with **Pubs of Portland** ($30, www.pubsofportlandtours.com). Since it's Portland, you can even group-pedal to local breweries on the **BrewCycle** ($25, www.brewgrouppdx.com) or bring your own brewskies and group-pedal on the Willamette River via the **BrewBarge** ($35, www.brewgrouppdx.com/brewbarge).

(11am and 12:30pm). *955 N. Russell St. (at Mississippi Ave.).* ☎ *503/281-2437. www.widmerbrothers.com. MAX: Albina/Mississippi. Map p 114.*

Cabaret

★★ Darcelle XV Showplace

DOWNTOWN   This campy cross-dressing cabaret has been going since 1967 and stars Darcelle, listed in the Guinness Book of Records as the oldest performing drag queen in the United States. Get ready for flashy numbers, insult comedy, naughty jokes, and bachelorette partiers. Shows Wednesday to Saturday. *208 NW 3rd Ave. (at Davis St.).* ☎ *503/222-5338. www.darcelle xv.com. Cover $20. MAX: Old Town/Chinatown. Bus: 4, 8, 9, 16, 35, 44, or 77. Map p 114.*

Dance Clubs

★★★ The Embers Avenue

OLD TOWN   The old dividing line between gay and straight gets blurred at the Embers Avenue, where everyone comes to dance under flashing lights until the wee hours. *110 NW Broadway.* ☎ *503/222-3082. www.facebook.com/EmbersAvenue. Cover $5–$7 weekends. Bus: 12. Map p 114.*

★★ The Escape Nightclub

DOWNTOWN   Portland's best dance-club experience is an alcohol-free, all-ages, gay-centric extravaganza, open only on Friday and Saturday nights, with floor shows at 2am. The best sound and light system in the city. *333 SW Park Ave. (btw. SW Oak & SW Stark).* ☎ *503/227-0830. Cover $10–$15. Fri–Sat only. Bus: 12. Map p 114.*

★★ Lola's Room DOWNTOWN

This cozy dance spot on the second floor of the historic McMenamin's Crystal Ballroom features DJs and live bands. *1332 W. Burnside.* ☎ *503/225-0047. Cover varies. Streetcar: Providence Park. Bus: 20. Map p 114.*

Gay & Lesbian Bars & Clubs

★★ CC Slaughter's OLD

TOWN   Popular with a young gay crowd, but definitely hetero-friendly, this nightclub and martini lounge spins different sounds every night of the week. *219 NW Davis St.* ☎ *503/248-9135. www.ccslaughters pdx.com. MAX: Old Town/Chinatown. Bus: 4, 8, 9, 16. Map p 114.*

★★ Crush Bar INNER SOUTH-

EAST   Gay-owned and operated, Crush Bar Is a restaurant/bar/events space that welcomes everyone and offers DJs, dancing, and burlesque shows throughout the week. *1400 SE Morrison St.* ☎ *503/235-8150. www. crushbar.com. Bus: 12. Map p 114.*

Drag night at The Embers Avenue.

★ **Scandals** DOWNTOWN The only remaining downtown gay bar-restaurant, Scandals has been going strong for over 35 years. It has a DJ booth, pool table, dartboard, and great people-watching. Live local bands and special events on Thursday. *1125 SW Stark St. (at 11th Ave.).* ☎ *503/227-5887. www. scandalspdx.com. Bus: 20. Streetcar: SW 10th & Stark. Map p 114.*

Live Jazz & Blues

★★ **Living Room Theaters** DOWNTOWN On weekends from 8pm to midnight, the front lounge of this unique movie theatre becomes an intimate venue for live jazz performed by a top-notch array of performers. *341 SW 10th Ave. (at Stark St.).* ☎ *971/222-2010. http:// pdx.livingroomtheaters.com. No cover. Bus: 20. Streetcar: SW 10th & Stark. Map p 114.*

★★ **Solae's Lounge** ALBERTA Southern cookin', good drinks, and groovy jazz makes Solae's a standout in jazz-challenged Portland. *1801 NE Alberta St.* ☎ *503/206-8338. www.solaeslounge.com. MAX: N. Killingsworth St. Map p 114.*

Martini Bars

★★★ **Olive or Twist** NORTHWEST More than just a clever name, this friendly Northwest martini bar serves up classic cocktails, single-malt scotches, and a seemingly endless variety of martinis (try the orange blossom). *925 NW 11th Ave. (at Lovejoy St.).* ☎ *503/546-2900. www.oliveortwistmartinibar. com. Streetcar: NW Lovejoy & 13th. Map p 114.*

★★ **Vault Martini Bar** PEARL House-made lavender-infused vodka and Marvin Gaye on the stereo are just the tip of the iceberg at this fashionable Pearl watering hole. It's small and can get crowded on weekends with prowling singles.

226 NW 12th Ave. (at Everett St.). ☎ *503/224-4909. Streetcar: NW 11th & Everett. Map p 114.*

Other

★ **Bula Kava House** CLINTON Portland's first kava house serves the mildly narcotic South Pacific beverage in coconut shells. Kava is definitely an acquired taste, but it's quite relaxing (and legal and non-addictive), an alternative social lubricant. *3115 SE Division St. (at 32nd Ave.).* ☎ *503/477-7823. Bus: 4. Map p 114.*

★★ **Ground Kontrol Classic Arcade** CHINATOWN Tired of the same old bar scene? Come here for two floors of classic arcade games and pinball machines, along with a full bar, and DJs in the evenings. *511 NW Couch St. (at 6th Ave.).* ☎ *503/796-9364. www. groundkontrol.com. Free admission. MAX: NW 5th & Couch St. Map p 114.*

Sports Bars

★★ **Life of Riley** PEARL Come cheer the Trail Blazers, Red Sox, or whoever else is playing (well, maybe not the Yankees) at this hard-drinking tavern, a welcome touch of blue collar in the

Live music at Ground Kontrol Classic Arcade.

Distillery Row

As if this town needed another alcoholic beverage to excel in, recently 11 microdistilleries have sprung up along "Distillery Row" on SE 7th and 9th avenues, south of Belmont Street. Places like **House Spirits Distillery** (65 SE Washington St.; www.housespirits. com; ☎ 503/235-3174) and **New Deal Distillery** (1311 SE 9th Ave.; www.newdealdistillery.com; ☎ 503/234-2513) craft small batches of everything from classic gins and brandies to coffee rum and pepper-infused vodka. Most offer tours and tastings. You can take a pedicab tour ($60) or get a $20 "passport" that covers tasting fees and includes discounts at nearby merchants. More information: www.proofpdx.com.

House Spirits on Distillery Row.

white-collar Pearl. *300 NW 10th Ave. (at Everett St.).* ☎ *503/224-1680. www.lifeofrileytavern.com. Streetcar: NW 10th & Everett. Map p 114.*

★★ Spirit of '77 NORTHEAST Named for the year the Portland Trail Blazers won the NBA championship, this place has high beamed ceilings, a 16-foot-high projection TV, free basketball hoops, and indoor bike parking. *500 NE Martin Luther King Jr. Blvd. (at Lloyd Blvd.).* ☎ *503/232-9977. www.spiritof77 bar.com. Bus: 6. Map p 114.*

Wine Bars

★★ Noble Rot SOUTHEAST On the third floor of the red "Rocket" buildings on East Burnside, this wine bar offers wine flights, great views of the city from a glassed-in patio, and dishes using produce from their rooftop garden. *1111 E. Burnside St. (at 11th Ave.).* ☎ *503/233-1999. www.noblerot pdx.com. Bus: 12, 19, or 20. Map p 114.* ●

The Best Arts & Entertainment

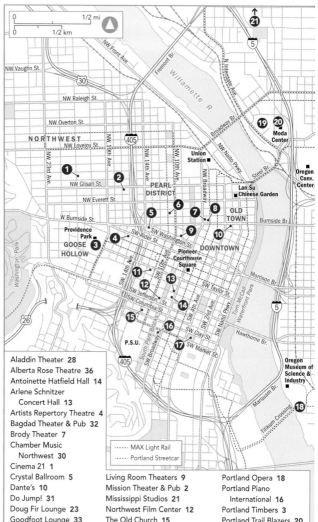

----- MAX Light Rail
----- Portland Streetcar

Previous page: Popular music at the Crystal Ballroom.

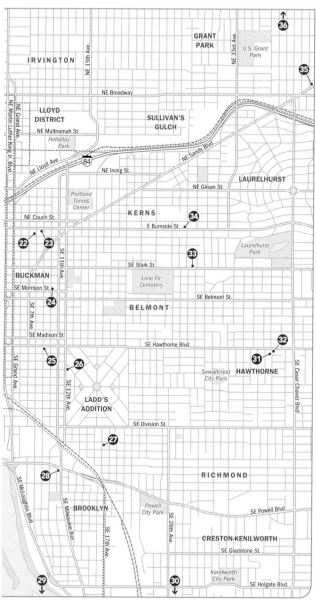

Arts & Entertainment Best Bets

Best for a **Beer During a Movie**
★★ Laurelhurst Theater,
2735 E. Burnside St. (p 129)

Best **Family Entertainment**
★★ Do Jump!, *1515 SE 37th Ave.*
(p 128)

Best for **Most Interesting Contemporary Dance**
★★★ PDX Contemporary Ballet,
1734 SE 12th Ave. (p 129)

Best **Rock Music Venue**
★★★ Doug Fir Lounge,
830 E. Burnside St. (p 131)

Best Place to **Shake Your Booty**
★★ Goodfoot Lounge,
2845 SE Stark St. (p 131)

Best **Classical Piano Recitals**
★★★ Portland Piano International, *1620 SW Park (p 127)*

Best for **Avant-Garde Films**
★★ Northwest Film Center,
1219 SW Park Ave. (p 130)

Best **Orchestra**
★★★ Oregon Symphony,
1037 SW Broadway (p 127)

Best for an **Unpredictable Performance**
★ Imago Theatre, *17 SE 8th Ave.*
(p 132)

Best **Chamber Music Performances**
★★★ Chamber Music Northwest,
3203 SE Woodstock Blvd. (p 127)

Best for a **Belly Laugh**
★★ Helium, *1510 SE 9th Ave.*
(p 128)

Best Place to be **Drafted into the Timbers Army**
★ Providence Park,
1844 SW Morrison St. (p 128)

Best **Rough-and-Tumble Entertainment**
★ Rose City Rollers,
7805 SE Oaks Park Way.
(p 132)

Ticket Deals

If you're willing to wait until the day of the show, you can get some good deals on tickets at places like **Portland Center Stage,** which offers any unsold tickets right before curtain time for $20. Many other theaters also offer day-of-performance rush tickets; check with the theater's website or call the box office for more details. At the Keller Auditorium, the **Portland Opera** offers unsold tickets to students and active military personnel for $10 and seniors for $20. The **Portland Center for the Performing Arts** has a day-of-show ticket hotline (☎ 503/432-2960) for performances at the Arlene Schnitzer Concert Hall, Antoinette Hatfield Hall, and Keller Auditorium.

Arts & Entertainment A to Z

Classical Music

★★★ Chamber Music Northwest EASTMORELAND One of the country's oldest chamber music organizations brings a year-round roster of renowned artists to perform at Reed College's Kaul Auditorium and other venues throughout the city. Check website for concert locations. *3203 SE Woodstock Blvd. (& other locations).* ☎ *503-223-3202. www.cmnw.org. Ticket prices vary. Bus: 19. Map p 124.*

★★★ Oregon Symphony DOWNTOWN Under the baton of music director Carlos Kalmar, the oldest symphony orchestra on the West Coast has become one of the country's top ensembles. Performances are at the Arlene Schnitzer Concert Hall (Sept–May). *1037 SW Broadway (at Main St.).* ☎ *503-228-4294. www.orsymphony.org. Tickets $20–$100. MAX: SW 6th & Madison sts. Bus: 8, 9, 10, 14, 17, or 66. Map p 124.*

★★★ Portland Baroque Orchestra DOWNTOWN Under the inspired leadership of Monica Huggett, this ensemble performs baroque and classical music composed before 1840, often on original instruments, at the First Baptist Church (on Sundays at Reed College's Kaul Auditorium). *909 SW 11th Ave. (at Taylor St.).* ☎ *503-222-6000. www.pbo.org. Tickets $25–$60. Streetcar: SW 11th & Taylor. Map p 124.*

★★★ Portland Piano International Up-and-coming stars of the keyboard perform solo recitals in Lincoln Hall at Portland State University. Hear them before they reach Carnegie Hall. *Lincoln Hall (PSU), 1620 SW Park (at Market).* ☎ *503-228-1388. www.portland piano.org. Tickets $25–$100. Streetcar: SW Park & Market. Map p 124.*

★★★ Third Angle New Music DIFFERENT VENUES The venues, the artists, and the music change for every performance by this "anything but ordinary" group devoted to contemporary music in all its guises. You might hear chamber music played on front porches of historic homes in Irvington, new Japanese music performed in the Portland Japanese Garden, or Phillip Glass works in a furniture design showroom. The caliber of the performances and the inventive musical programming never fails to attract an enthusiastic and engaged audience. Check website for performance locations and ticket info; *No fixed street address; every*

Carlos Kalmar conducts the Oregon Symphony.

The Best Arts & Entertainment

performance at a different venue. ☎ 503/331-0301. www.thirdangle. org. Ticket prices vary.

Comedy Clubs

★ **Brody Theater** CHINATOWN Swing by for a stand-up or improv show or an avant-garde theater production; come back later and take a class. *16 NW Broadway (at Burnside).* ☎ 503/224-2227. www. brodytheater.com. Tickets $8–$12. MAX: SW 6th & Pine St. Bus: 1, 12, 19, 20, 54, or 56. Map p 124.

★★ **Helium** INNER SOUTHEAST Local and national stand-up acts appear at this slick comedy club. *1510 SE 9th Ave. (at Hawthorne Blvd.).* ☎ 888/643-8669. www.helium comedy.com. Tickets $5–$35, 2-item minimum. Bus: 10 or 14. Map p 124.

Concert & Event Venues

★★ **Alberta Rose Theatre** ALBERTA Catch some live music, an independent film, or a taping of the *Live Wire!* radio show at this 300-seat restored 1927 movie house. *3000 NE Alberta St. (at 30th Ave.).* ☎ 503/719-6055. www. albertarosetheatre.com. Tickets $15–$30. Bus: 72. Map p 124.

★★ **Antoinette Hatfield Hall** DOWNTOWN This postmodern building encloses two theaters: the larger Newmark and more versatile Dolores Winningstad, hosting plays, dance, music, films, and more. *1111 SW Broadway (at 11th Ave.).* ☎ 503/248-4335. www.pcpa.com. Ticket prices vary. MAX: SW 6th & Madison St. Bus: 8, 9, 10, 14, 17, or 66. Map p 124.

★★★ **Arlene Schnitzer Concert Hall** DOWNTOWN The crown jewel of the Portland Center for the Performing Arts, the "Schnitz" is the city's most lavish performance space, home to the Oregon Symphony and a year-round roster of top performers and performances. *1037 SW Broadway (at Main St.).* ☎ 503/248-4335. www.pcpa.com. Ticket prices vary. MAX: SW 6th & Madison St. Bus: 8, 9, 10, 14, 17, or 66. Map p 124.

★★ **Keller Auditorium** DOWNTOWN The 3,000-seat Keller is where groups like **Portland Opera** and the **Oregon Ballet Theatre** perform (they use other venues as well), and which serves as a venue for traveling Broadway shows. *222 SW Clay St.* www.portland5.com/keller-auditorium. Ticket prices vary. Map p 124.

★★★ **The Old Church** DOWNTOWN Every Wednesday at noon, this 1883 Carpenter Gothic landmark hosts free "sack lunch" concerts of classical music by local artists. Other concerts and events through the year. Also see p 45. *1422 SW 11th Ave.* ☎ 503/222-2031. www.oldchurch.org. Free admission. Streetcar: SW 11th & Clay. Map p 124.

★★★ **Providence Park** DOWNTOWN This historic open-air stadium hosted Elvis and 14,000 screaming fans in 1957; now it's home base for the Portland State University Vikings football team and the Portland Timbers MLS team (see p 131). *1844 SW Morrison St. (at 18th Ave.).* ☎ 503/553-5400. www. providenceparkpdx.com. Ticket prices vary. MAX: Providence Park. Bus: 15, 20. Map p 124.

Dance

★★★ **kids** **Do Jump!** HAWTHORNE With energetic performances that are as much aerial acrobatics as dance, this inventive local company always puts on a good show. *1515 SE 37th Ave. (at Hawthorne Blvd.).* ☎ 503/231-1232. www.dojump.org. Ticket prices vary. Bus: 14. Map p 124.

★★ **Oregon Ballet Theatre** DOWNTOWN This company,

White Bird hosts international dance companies such as Momix.

founded in 1989, performs both classical (including a yearly *Nutcracker*) and modern ballet at the Newmark Theatre in Antoinette Hatfield Hall (see p 128) and the Keller Auditorium (222 SW Clay St.) *1111 SW Broadway (at 11th Ave).* ☎ *503/222-5538. www.obt.org. Tickets $25–$140. MAX: SW 6th & Madison St. Bus: 8, 9, 10, 14, 17, or 66. Map p 124.*

★★★ PDX Contemporary Ballet INNER SOUTHEAST
This young company synthesizes contemporary and classical ballet movement to create riveting original performances. Every show premieres new choreography. Check website for performance locations. *1734 SE 12th Ave. Tickets $25–$30. Bus: 15. Streetcar: Grand & Belmont. Map p 124.*

★★ White Bird DOWNTOWN
Fans of international modern dance should check out what's being produced by White Bird. Venues change but the main performance site is Arlene Schnitzer Concert Hall. *1037 SW Broadway.* ☎ *503/245-1600. www.whitebird.org. Ticket prices vary. Bus: 8, 9, 10, 14, 17, or 66. Map p 124.*

Film

★★★ kids Bagdad Theater & Pub HAWTHORNE
This 1927 theater with a pub and two bars shows second-run movies for cheap, along with offbeat performances. *3702 SE Hawthorne Blvd.* ☎ *503/467-7521. www.mcmenamins.*

com. Ticket prices vary. Bus: 14. Map p 124.

★★ Cinema 21 NORTHWEST
One of Portland's most beloved movie theaters shows shorts, documentaries, and critically acclaimed features that won't make it to the multiplex. *616 NW 21st Ave. (at Irving St.).* ☎ *503/223-4515. www.cinema21.com. Tickets $8–$10. Bus: 17. Map p 124.*

★★ Hollywood Theatre HOLLYWOOD
The city's most ornate classic theater retains its 1926 Byzantine rococo facade and shows first- and second-run independent and foreign films and vintage classics. *4122 NE Sandy Blvd. (at 41st Ave.).* ☎ *503/281-4215. www.hollywoodtheatre.org. Tickets $5–$10. Bus: 12. Map p 124.*

★★ Laurelhurst Theater LAURELHURST
Pizza, salads, microbrews, and second-run flicks fill the bill at this restored 1923 theater with a vintage neon sign. *2735 E. Burnside St. (at 28th Ave.).* ☎ *503/232-5511. www.laurelhursttheater.com. Tickets $5–$10. Bus: 20. Map p 124.*

★★ Living Room Theaters DOWNTOWN
Combine a European lounge and cafe with an independent theater and you get the chicest eat-in-your-seat movie house in town. You can order drinks and meals that will delivered to your seat. *341 SW 10th Ave. (at Stark St.).* ☎ *971/222-2010.*

http://pdx.livingroomtheaters.com.
Tickets $8–$10. Bus: 20. Streetcar:
SW 10th & Stark. Map p 124.

★★ Mission Theater & Pub

NORTHWEST This former church
and longshoreman's union hall
combines an ever-changing program of second-run and vintage
films and cabaret shows with beer
and pub grub; one of the first of its
kind. 1624 NW St. (at 17th Ave.).
☎ 503/223-4527. www.
mcmenamins.com. Tickets $5–$8.
Bus: 20. Map p 124.

★★ Northwest Film Center

DOWNTOWN The Portland Art
Museum's Whitsell Auditorium
hosts classic, experimental, ani-
mated, foreign, and indie films,
plus film festivals and work by local
filmmakers. 1219 SW Park Ave. (at
Madison St.). ☎ 503/221-1156, ext.
10. www.nwfilm.org. Tickets $8–$10.
Streetcar: Art Museum. Map p 124.

Opera

★★ Portland Opera INNER

EASTSIDE The Rose City's opera
company puts on five productions
(Sept–Mar) at Hampton Opera Cen-
ter and at Keller Auditorium (222
SW Clay St.), including works by
Puccini, Mozart, Verdi, Wagner,
Strauss, Leonard Bernstein, and
Philip Glass. 211 SE Caruthers St.

☎ 503/241-1407. www.portland
opera.org. Tickets $45–$150. Streetcar: SE Water/OMSI. Map p 124.

Popular Music

★★★ Aladdin Theater SOUTH-

EAST This 1920s vaudeville house
is now a stellar mid-size performance
hall for live music from Emmylou Har-
ris to Maceo Parker and Ryan Adams.
3017 SE Milwaukie Ave. ☎ 503/233-
1994. www.aladdin-theater.com. Tickets $10–$45. Bus: 9, 17, 19, 66, or 70.
Map p 124.

★★★ Crystal Ballroom DOWN-

TOWN When's the last time you
rocked out on the floating-on-ball-
bearings dance floor of a 1914 ballroom? Jimi Hendrix, James Brown,
and the Grateful Dead all played at
this historic and much-loved local
institution; Rudolf Valentino did the
tango here in the 1920s. 1332 W.
Burnside St. (at 14th Ave.). ☎ 503/
225-0047. www.danceonair.com.
Ticket prices vary. Bus: 20. Map p 124.

★ Dante's OLD TOWN The Sin-

ferno Cabaret, Karaoke From Hell,
live bands, and DJs make this club
a tempting destination for a night
of dancing and debauchery. 350 W.
Burnside St. (at 5th Ave.). ☎ 503/
226-6630. www.danteslive.com.
Cover free to $20. Bus: 12, 19, or 20.
Map p 124.

The Portland Opera performs at Keller Auditorium.

Rocking out at the Doug Fir Lounge.

★★★ **Doug Fir Lounge** INNER SOUTHEAST Attached to the Jupiter Hotel, the Doug Fir features alt-rock and great acoustics. *830 E. Burnside St. (at 9th Ave.).* ☎ *503/231-9663. www.dougfirlounge.com. Cover $10–$25. Bus: 12, 19, or 20. Map p 124.*

★★ **Goodfoot Lounge** LAUREL-HURST Get up offa that thing and shake it to jazz, funk, soul, Afro-beat, and everything in between. *2845 SE Stark St. (at 29th Ave.).* ☎ *503/239-9292. www.thegood foot.com. Cover free to $10. Bus: 15. Map p 124.*

★★ **Holocene** SOUTHEAST Theme nights and a roster of local and national singers and bands perform at this nightclub with two stages, a dance floor, and cheap covers. *1001 SE Morrison St. (at 10th Ave.).* ☎ *503/239-7639. www.holocene.org. Cover $5–$10. Bus: 15. Map p 124.*

★★ **Mississippi Studios** MISSISSIPPI This venue in the heart of the historic Mississippi District caters to people who actually want to *listen* to live music in an intimate setting. Good acoustics, and free shows once a month. *3939 N. Mississippi Ave. (at Shaver St.).* ☎ *503/288-3895. www.mississippi studios.com. Cover free to $20. Bus: 4. Map p 124.*

★ **Roseland Theater** CHINA-TOWN Not the most pleasant live-music venue, but one of the few non-stadium places to see major rock acts. *8 NW 6th Ave. (at Burnside St.).* ☎ *503/224-8499. www. roselandpdx.com. Ticket prices vary. Bus: 9, 17, 20, 54, or 56. Map p 124.*

Sports

★★★ **Portland Timbers** DOWNTOWN The Major League Soccer team fills Providence Park stadium with the howls of the "Timbers Army" (Mar–Oct). *1844 SW Morrison St. (at 18th Ave.).* ☎ *503/553-5400. www.portlandtimbers.com. Tickets $18–$35. MAX: Providence Park. Map p 124.*

★★ **Portland Trail Blazers** ROSE QUARTER The Northwest's only NBA team last won the championship in 1977, but they still sell out the 20,000-seat Moda Center arena (Nov–Apr). *1 Center Court.* ☎ *503/234-9291. www.nba.com/blazers. Tickets average $60. MAX: Moda Center. Map p 124.*

A performance of The Lost Boy *at Artists Repertory Theatre.*

★ **Portland Winterhawks** ROSE QUARTER This junior hockey team, part of the Western Hockey League, counts Hall of Famers Cam Neely and Mark Messier among its NHL alumni (Memorial Coliseum, Sept–Mar). *300 N. Winning Way.* ☎ *503/238-6366. www.winterhawks. com. Tickets $15–$55. MAX: Moda Center. Map p 124.*

★★ **Rose City Rollers** SELLWOOD The Breakneck Betties and the Axles of Annihilation are two of the six teams that make up this all-female amateur roller derby league. Catch an exciting (and unscripted) bout at Oaks Park in Sellwood, and occasionally at Memorial Coliseum or the Portland Expo Center (Jan–June). *7805 SE Oaks Park Way.* ☎ *503/784-1444. www.rosecityrollers.com. Tickets $16–$25. Bus: 70. Map p 124.*

Theater

★★ **Artists Repertory Theatre** DOWNTOWN More challenging contemporary productions and premieres, along with works by established playwrights like Harold Pinter and David Mamet, come courtesy of this first-rate company. Their big-red-box theater is an informal, intimate setting. *1516 SW Alder St. (at 16th Ave.).* ☎ *503/241-1278. www. artistsrep.org. Tickets $10–$50. MAX:* *Providence Park. Bus: 15, 20. Map p 124.*

★★★ kids **Imago Theatre** INNER SOUTHEAST You never know what a night with Imago holds—physical comedy, animal costumes, mime, dance, acrobatics, music—but it definitely will be interesting. Productions like Frogz, ZooZoo, and Splat are as entertaining to kids as they are to their parents. *17 SE 8th Ave. (at Burnside St.).* ☎ *503/231-9581. www.imago theatre.com. Ticket prices vary. Bus: 12, 19, or 20. Map p 124.*

★★ **Portland Center Stage** PEARL The Gerding Theater at the Armory is home of the city's largest professional theater company, performing classic and contemporary works and musicals (Sept–June). *128 NW 11th Ave. (at Davis St.).* ☎ *503/445-3700. www. pcs.org. Tickets $20–$75. Streetcar: 10th & Couch. Bus: 12, 19, or 20. Map p 124.*

★ **Theatre Vertigo** BELMONT Performing at the Shoebox Theater, this talented company puts on intriguing ensemble performances of new, old, and ongoing works as well as readings. *110 SE 10th Ave.* ☎ *503/306-0870. www.theatre vertigo.org. Tickets $15. Bus: 15. Map p 124.* ●

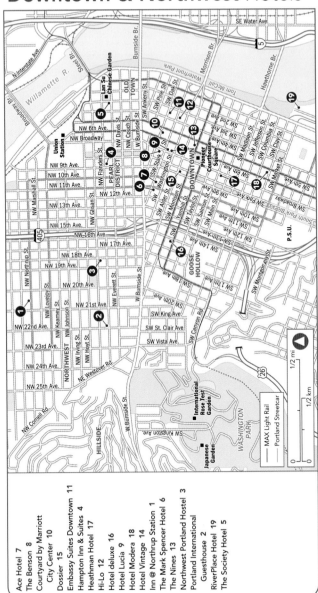

Previous page: The Hi-Lo Hotel.

East Side Hotels

Jupiter Hotel **3**
Lion and the Rose Victorian B&B **2**
McMenamins Kennedy School **1**
Portland Mayor's Mansion **4**

Hotel **Best Bets**

Best for **Families**
★ Embassy Suites Downtown $$$
319 SW Pine St. (p 138)

Best **Value**
★★ The Society Hotel $
203 NW 3rd Ave. (p 140)

Best **Historic B & B**
★★★ Portland Mayor's Mansion
$$ *3360 SE Ankeny St. (p 140)*

Best **Splurge**
★★★ The Nines $$$
525 SW Morrison St. (p 139)

Best for **Romance**
★★★ Dossier $$$
750 SW Alder St. (p 137)

Best **Service**
★★ Heathman Hotel $$$
1001 SW Broadway (p 138)

Best **Unusual Vibe**
★★★ McMenamins Kennedy
School $$ *5736 NE 33rd Ave. (p 139)*

Best **Hotel Bar & Restaurant**
★★★ Hotel Vintage $$$
422 SW Broadway (p 139)

Best **Hip Vibe**
★★★ Hi-Lo $$$ *320 SW Stark St.*
(p 138)

Best for **Willamette River Views**
★★ RiverPlace Hotel $$$
1510 SW Harbor Way (p 140)

Best for **Traditional Elegance**
★★★ The Benson $
309 SW Broadway (p 137)

Best for **Live Music**
★ Jupiter Hotel $
800 E. Burnside (p 139)

The Bacchus Bar and spiral staircase at Hotel Vintage.

Hotels A to Z

★★ Ace Hotel DOWNTOWN
Stylish from the photo booth in the lobby to the turntables in the rooms, the Ace is a short walk from Powell's City of Books and is surprisingly affordable, befitting a hip young clientele (and their pets). *1022 SW Stark St.* ☎ *503/228-2277. www. acehotel.com. $125–$175 w/shared bath, $162–$245 w/private bath. Self-park $34. Pets accepted. Streetcar: SW 10th & Stark. Map p 134.*

★★★ The Benson DOWNTOWN
Since 1912, the Benson has topped Portland's old-world-charm category, now updated with Tempur-Pedic mattresses. Put it this way: Presidents stay here when they come to town. *309 SW Broadway.* ☎ *888/523-6766 or 503/228-2000. www.bensonhotel. com. 287 units. Doubles $150–$254. Valet parking $40. Pets accepted. MAX: SW 5th & Oak. Map p 134.*

★ Courtyard by Marriott City Center DOWNTOWN   A solid midrange option in the heart of the city, this Courtyard was freshly created from a former office building and has a friendly, contemporary feel. *550 SW Oak St.* ☎ *800/ 606-3717 or 503/505-5000. www. myfavoritecourtyard.com. 256 units. Doubles $188–$261. MAX: SW 5th & Oak. Map p 134.*

★★★ Dossier DOWNTOWN
Opened in 2017, this centrally located downtown hotel combines traditional comfort with sophisticated flair. Roomy rooms feature big windows, big city views, natural wood and stone finishes, and photographs by Slim Aarons. Opal Café and Bar, the hotel's restaurant, serves crafty craft cocktails and Pacific Northwest cuisine. *750 SW Alder St. www.dossierhotel.com.* ☎ *877/628-4408 or 503/294-9000.*

The Portland Hotel Scene

The hotel scene, like every other scene in Portland, has changed dramatically in the last ten years. The city used to be plain Jane when it came to lodging, but now it has a number of stylish, comfortable hotels at all levels of sophistication, with more opening all the time, as well as intriguing B&Bs and hostels. The prices listed are for a double room in low season (winter) and high season (July–Aug).
  Travel Portland, 701 SW Sixth Ave., Portland, OR 97205 (www. travelportland.com; ☎ **877/678-5263** or 503/275-9293) provides a hotel reservation service for the Portland metro area. For information on **B&Bs** in the Portland area, contact the **Oregon Bed & Breakfast Guild** (www.obbg.org; ☎ **800/944-6196**). Rental options in private homes can be found on sites like **Airbnb** (www. airbnb.com), **HomeAway** (www.homeaway.com), and **VRBO** (www. vrbo.com). These websites, offering rooms in private homes and sometimes entire apartments, are legal to use in Portland and offer accommodations that are typically $25 to $50 less than what you'd pay for a hotel room just about anywhere in Portland.

Opal Café and Bar at the Dossier Hotel.

205 units. Doubles $200–$380. Valet parking $33. Pets accepted. MAX: Pioneer Courthouse Sq. Streetcar: SW 10th & Alder. Map p 134.

★ kids **Embassy Suites Downtown** DOWNTOWN Mostly two-room suites, perfect for families, fill this historic property. Enjoy a good free breakfast, complimentary evening cocktails, and walk to everything in downtown. *319 SW Pine St.* ☎ 800/EMBASSY [362-2779] or 503/279-9000. www.embassy portland.com. 276 units. Doubles $160–$270 w/full breakfast. Valet parking $45; self-parking $35 MAX: SW 5th & Oak. Map p 134.

★★ kids **Hampton Inn & Suites** PEARL DISTRICT This moderately priced Hilton-brand hotel opened in 2017 and offers large, comfortable rooms without a lot of high-end frills. But the lodging has a big indoor swimming pool with water features that the kids will love, and a roof patio with views out over the city. Tanner Creek Tavern is right off the lobby. *354 NW Ninth Ave.* ☎ 800/426-7866 or 503/222-5200. www.portlandpearldistrict.hampton byhilton.com. 243 units. Doubles $152–$220. Valet parking $37. Streetcar: NW 10th & Glisan. Map p 134.

★★ **Heathman Hotel** DOWNTOWN Adjacent to "the Schnitz" concert hall, you'll find a first-rate place with classic service and modern amenities, from in-room French press coffeemakers to a library full of signed first editions. *1001 SW Broadway.* ☎ 800/551-0011 or 503/241-4100. http://portland.heathmanhotel.com.

150 units. Doubles $219–$450. Bus: 15 or 31. Map p 134.

★★★ **Hi-Lo** DOWNTOWN This unique and stylishly hip hotel opened in 2017 in the 1910 Oregon Pioneer Building. Spacious rooms make use of the building's original concrete and steel-beam construction, and have large bathrooms with big walk-in rain showers. Alto Bajo (p 100), the hotel's excellent restaurant, serves modern Mexican cuisine. *320 SW Stark St.* www.hi-lo-hotel.com. ☎ 971/222-2100. 120 units. Doubles $197–$275. Valet parking $39. Pets accepted. MAX: SW 2nd & Oak. Map p 134.

★★ **Hotel deLuxe** DOWNTOWN Step into the Golden Age of Hollywood at this reinvented historic downtown hotel decorated with black-and-white photos of classic stars. Rooms can be snug, but they have a breezy LA aesthetic. The cozy Driftwood Room has been a Portland cocktail staple since the 1950s. *729 SW 15th Ave.* ☎ 866/986-8085 or 503/219-2094. www. hoteldeluxeportland.com. 103 units. Doubles $135–$279. Valet parking $33. Pets accepted. MAX: Providence Park. Map p 134.

★★★ **Hotel Lucía** DOWNTOWN Paintings by Northwest artists and photos by former White House photog David Hume Kennerly set an artsy, contemporary tone and draw a younger professional crowd (and their pets) to this cool, comfortable, centrally located downtown hotel. *400 SW Broadway.* ☎ 866/986-8086 or 503/225-1717. www.hotellucia.com.

128 units. Doubles $143–$271. Valet parking $43. Pets accepted. MAX: Oak/SW 1st. Map p 134.

★★★ Hotel Modera DOWN-TOWN

Outstanding eatery Nel Centro with its outdoor fire pits and vertical wall garden is just one facet of this stylish luxury boutique hotel fashioned from a 1950s motor lodge. *515 SW Clay St.* ☎ *503/484-1084. www.hotelmodera.com. 174 units. Doubles $119–$299. Valet parking $38. MAX: Mall/SW 5th. Map p 134.*

★★★ Hotel Vintage DOWN-TOWN

This historic, hotel, built in 1894, was completely redone in 2017 to make it one of the hippest and most wine-scenic of downtown Portland hotels. Book one of the atelier-like rooms, or one with an outdoor hot tub, and enjoy a free evening wine tasting in Bacchus, the trendy lobby bar. The Italian restaurant Pazzo is on hand when you get hungry. *422 SW Broadway.* ☎ *800/263-2305 or 503/228-1212. www.hotelvintage-portland.com. 117 units. Doubles $166–$336. Valet parking $43. Pets accepted. MAX: Pioneer Sq. Map p 134.*

★★ Inn @ Northrup Station

NORTHWEST A colorful retro retreat right on the streetcar line, this all-suite boutique hotel has lots of rooms with balconies and make-your-own waffles for breakfast. Quirky décor, super-friendly staff, interesting neighborhood. *2025 NW Northrup St.* ☎ *800/224-1180 or 503/224-0543. www.northrupstation. 70 units. Doubles $139–$239 w/continental breakfast. Free parking. Streetcar: NW Northrup & 22nd. Map p 134.*

★ Jupiter Hotel SOUTHEAST

You may feel like an indie rock star, or an old fogey, at this youth-centric hotel-entertainment-complex fashioned from a motor lodge—and you can catch a real rock star at the attached Doug Fir Lounge. A new addition in 2017 offers quieter and more comfort-conscious rooms. *800 E. Burnside St.* ☎ *877/800-0004 or 503/230-9200. www.jupiterhotel.com. 148 units. $139–$199 double. Parking $15. Pets accepted. Bus: 12, 19, or 20. Map p 135.*

★★ Lion and the Rose Victorian B&B Inn IRVINGTON

This 1905 Queen Anne house is stocked with antiques and claw-foot tubs, but the best part may be what's outside: a beautiful rose garden and the eminently walkable Irvington neighborhood. *1810 NE 15th Ave.* ☎ *800/955-1647 or 503/287-9245. www.lionrose.com. 8 units. Doubles $100–$240 w/breakfast. Bus: 8. Map p 135.*

★ kids The Mark Spencer Hotel DOWNTOWN

This favorite downtown budget choice for extended stays features clean, comfortable rooms with kitchenettes, breakfast, and a complimentary evening wine hour. *409 SW 11th Ave.* ☎ *800/548-3934 or 503/224-3293. www.markspencer.com. 102 units. $169–$249 double w/continental breakfast. Parking $20. Pets accepted. MAX: Galleria/SW 10th. Map p 134.*

★★★ kids McMenamins Kennedy School ALBERTA

Sleep in a former schoolroom, complete with blackboard, or just roam the art-paneled halls of this former elementary school, probably the most intriguing lodging in town. Restaurants, bars, movie theater, and soaking pool on site. *5736 NE 33rd Ave.* ☎ *888/249-3983 or 503/249-3983. www.mcmeneminscom/427-kennedy-school-home. 57 units. Doubles $195–$235. Pets accepted. Bus: 73. Map p 135.*

★★★ The Nines DOWNTOWN

From its eighth-floor atrium lobby to its rooftop Departure Lounge, the Nines is fun, fashionable, and full-service; rooms have a turquoise-and-white color scheme and great

The former Portland Mayor's Mansion is now a classic B&B.

downtown city views. Urban Farmer is a farm-to-fork steakhouse. *525 SW Morrison St.* ☎ *877/229-9995 or 503/715-1738. www.thenines.com. 331 units. Doubles $228–$413. Valet parking $47. Pets accepted. MAX: Pioneer Courthouse. Map p 134.*

★★ Northwest Portland Hostel

NORTHWEST This Hostel International (HI) complex consists of five adjacent properties clustered around an outdoor courtyard-lounge area. There are endless sleeping configurations, including dorm rooms with bunk beds, private rooms, and cottages, all with en-suite bathrooms, shared kitchen, and commons area. Hostel Café is open late and the commons area and courtyard are open 24 hours a day. And best of all, you can easily walk or bike to just about anything in central Portland. *479 NW 18th Ave.* ☎ *503/241-2783. www.nwportlandhostel.com. 29 units, 156 dorm beds. Doubles $94–$114, dorm bed $31–$40. Streetcar: NW 18th & Lovejoy. Map p 134.*

★ Portland International Guesthouse

NORTHWEST Six spotless rooms share three full bathrooms at this friendly and inexpensive guesthouse in a quiet residential neighborhood. *2185 NW Flanders St.* ☎ *877/228-0500 or 503/224-0500. www.pdxguesthouse. com. 6 units. Doubles $75–$85, $110 apartment. Bus: 15. Streetcar: NW 21st & Lovejoy. Map p 134.*

★★★ Portland Mayor's Mansion

LAURELHURST Built in 1912 for a former mayor of Portland, this imposing Colonial Revival is a feast of period detail located right on historic Laurelhurst Park. It's the top-rated B&B in Portland for good reason. *3360 SE Ankeny St.* ☎ *503/232-3588. www.pdxmayors-mansion.com. 4 units. Doubles $175–$190 w/full breakfast, $280 suite. Bus: 75. Map p 135.*

★★ RiverPlace Hotel

DOWNTOWN The only truly riverside hotel downtown, this upscale, pet-friendly Kimpton property abuts Waterfront Park, has views of the Willamette, and provides guest bikes and a complimentary evening wine hour. *1510 SW Harbor Way.* ☎ *800/227-1333 or 503/228-3233. www.riverplacehotel.com. 84 units. Doubles $174–$403. Valet parking $37. Pets accepted. Streetcar: SW 1st & Harrison. Map p 134.*

★★★ The Society Hotel

OLD TOWN/CHINATOWN This combined hotel-hostel is the best hotel deal in Portland. It occupies a late-19th-century building and features small, well-designed rooms and coed dorm rooms with curtained bunk beds that have an outlet for recharging your phone, a reading light, and a comfortable mattress. There's a nice café and a terrific roof terrace with great city views. You can easily walk anywhere downtown. *203 NW 3rd Ave. www.thesocietyhotel.com.* ☎ *503/445-0444. 38 units, 24 bunks. Doubles $129–$169 w/private bath, $69–$109 w/shared bath; dorm bed $35–$55. MAX: Skidmore Fountain. Map p 134.* ●

Mount Hood

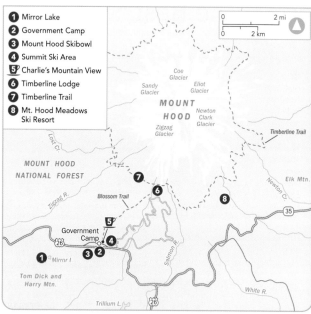

1. Mirror Lake
2. Government Camp
3. Mount Hood Skibowl
4. Summit Ski Area
5. Charlie's Mountain View
6. Timberline Lodge
7. Timberline Trail
8. Mt. Hood Meadows Ski Resort

Portland's snow-capped icon shimmers on the eastern horizon whenever the skies are clear. At 11,240 feet, Mount Hood is Oregon's highest point, with twelve glaciers above the classic Timberline Lodge. The mountain is an outdoor playground in any season, but especially in winter, when some spots get 500 inches of snow. U.S. 26, a National Scenic Byway, generally follows Barlow Road, the final and most difficult stretch of the Oregon Trail. START: Troutdale, I-84 exit 18, 17 miles east of Portland.

1 ★★ kids **Mirror Lake.** A trailhead on Hwy. 26 between mileposts 51 and 52 accesses an easy 1.6-mile trail to a picture-perfect lake with spectacular views of Mt. Hood. A Northwest Forest Pass ($5/day per car) is required to park at the trailhead.

2 ★ **Government Camp.** First settled in 1900, this tiny mountain resort community sits at the foot of Mt. Hood amid fir and cedar forests. It has a handful of restaurants, hotels, and rental condos, making it a good base in summer or winter.

3 ★★ kids **Mount Hood Skibowl.** The closest ski resort to Portland is also the country's largest night ski area, with 600 acres lit up after dark. The Cascade Express lift accesses popular cruising terrain and panoramic views from 7,300 feet. It's as much a summer

Previous page: Vista House at Crown Point, overlooking the Columbia River Gorge.

destination as a winter one, with an adventure park and mountain-bike rentals available in the summer. *87000 E. Hwy. 26, Government Camp.* ☎ *503/272-3206. www.skibowl.com. Lift tickets $53 adults, $49 children 6–12 & seniors 59 & over.*

4 ★★ kids **Summit Ski Area.** Also near Government Camp, the Northwest's first ski resort—opened in 1927—has a single lift and two downhill runs. It's a good place to learn, and it offers snow tubing and 10 miles of cross-country ski trails. *90255 E. Government Camp Loop, Government Camp.* ☎ *503/272-0256. www.summitskiarea.com. Lift tickets $30 adults, $20 children 6–12, free for seniors over 70 & kids 5 & under.*

What **5** **Charlie's Mountain View** lacks in ambience it makes up for in good food, such as the Mountain Cheese Burger with waffle fries, and the wide-window view of Mt. Hood. Check the conditions beforehand on their live webcam. *88462 E. Government Camp Loop, Government Camp.* ☎ *503/272-3333. www.charliesmountainview.com. $.*

6 ★★★ **Timberline Lodge.** Built as a WPA project in the 1930s and dedicated by President Franklin Roosevelt, this mountain lodge is full of classic Cascadian character, from its huge stone fireplace and glass tile mosaics to the extensive carved woodwork everywhere. At 6,060 feet on the shoulder of Mt. Hood, it has an unmatched view of the peak and, on clear days, 100 miles in almost every direction. The attached ski area, with 41 trails and nine lifts, is the only one in the country with year-round skiing. The lodge is a wonderfully atmospheric and romantic place to stay and offers fine dining in the **Cascade Dining Room** and casual fare in the **Ram's Head Bar.** *Timberline Hwy., Mt. Hood.* ☎ *800/547-1406 or 503/272-3410. www.timberlinelodge.com. Rooms $155–$385. Lift tickets $34–$76 adults, $31–$47 seniors, $5 kids 7–14.*

7 ★★★ **Timberline Trail.** You can take it 40.7 miles all the way around the mountain or just do part on a day hike, but either way this is one of Oregon's most scenic hiking trails, ranging from 3,200 to 7,300 feet in elevation. *Access from Timberline Lodge or Mount Hood Meadows. Snow-free mid-July through early Oct.*

8 ★★★ kids **Mt. Hood Meadows Ski Resort.** The biggest resort on the mountain is also one of the best in the Northwest for serious skiers, with 2,150 acres of wildly varied terrain, nine freestyle parks, and a full ski school. Locals know to head to Heather Canyon and Elk and Yoda Bowls on powder days. *14040 Hwy 35, 10 miles north of Government Camp.* ☎ *503/659-1256. www.skihood.com. Lift tickets $72–$82 adults, $59 seniors, $49 kids 7–14, $12 kids 7 & under.*

Snowcapped Mount Hood.

Columbia River Gorge

1 Historic Columbia River Highway
2 Crown Point and Vista House
3 Bridal Veil Falls
4 Multnomah Falls
5 Multnomah Falls Lounge
6 Triple waterfall hike
7 Bonneville Lock and Dam
8 Cascade Locks
9 Hood River
10 Hood River Valley Fruit Loop
11 The Dalles
12 Columbia Gorge Discovery Center and Museum

The Northwest's version of the Grand Canyon is 85 miles of basalt cliffs, lofty waterfalls, lush forests, and, oh yes, the seventh-longest river in the country. The Oregon side of the Gorge is a must-do day trip—or longer—from Portland. Combine it with Mt. Hood (p 142) for an even more impressive excursion. Please note: In 2017, the Eagle Creek wildfire burned more than 40,000 acres in the Gorge, but the most iconic sights were spared or saved. Be aware that some trails may be closed for restoration. START: Troutdale, OR, 17 miles east of Portland.

1 ★★★ Historic Columbia River Highway. The best (although not the fastest) way to experience the grandeur of the Columbia River Gorge is the way they did it in the days of Model Ts. Built between 1916 to 1926, the country's first scenic highway was designed as a way for car travelers to enjoy the magnificent scenery, and it was considered one of the great engineering feats of its time.

The narrow road winds for 70 miles along the southern side of the gorge, with dramatic climbs and descents and S-curves, past one amazing viewpoint, roaring waterfall, and 2,000-foot cliff to the next. Many of the original Florentine viaducts crafted by Italian stonecutters are still in place. Leave at least a few hours—better yet a whole day—from Troutdale to reach the Dalles (see p 149), or just Hood River (see

p 147). If you're in a hurry, I-84 also runs along the river. ☎ *541/308-1700. www.fs.usda.gov/crgnsa.*

❷ ★★★ **Crown Point and Vista House.** If the Columbia Gorge had a headquarters, it would be at Crown Point, with its 30-mile

views from atop a sheer 733-foot cliff. Here you'll find the unmistakable octagonal Vista House, built in 1918 as an observatory and rest stop. After a $3.2 million restoration, its resume expanded to include a museum, gift shop, and cafe. *3 miles east of Corbett on*

Vista House offers panoramic views of the Columbia River Gorge.

Historic Columbia River Hwy., I-84 exit 22. ☎ *503/695-2240. www.vista house.com. Daily Mar–Oct 10am–6pm, weather permitting. Free admission.*

❸ ★★ kids Bridal Veil Falls. Five miles east of Crown Point, Bridal Veil Creek tumbles down Larch Mountain and plunges into space, falling in two gauzy plumes for a total of 120 feet. Two trails leave from the picnic tables and restrooms at the parking lot. The short and easy lower trail heads down to the base, while a longer interpretive trail winds up to the lip of the falls. Both trails are under 1 mile round-trip. *Milepost 28 on Historic Columbia River Scenic Highway, I-84 exit 28.* ☎ *800/551-6949. Daily dawn–dusk. Free admission.*

❹ ★★★ kids Multnomah Falls. Oregon's highest cascade, and the second-highest year-round waterfall in the country plummets 620 feet in two tiers down a clef in Larch Mountain. It's a majestic sight, even though its tourist must-see status can bring big crowds on weekends. The scene is enhanced, or at least not marred, by the graceful curve of the Benson Footbridge, built in 1914 about 100 feet over the lower falls. It's part of a

Multnomah Falls.

1.2-mile trail that climbs 600 feet to the top of the upper falls, where an expansive panorama and the much smaller "Little Multnomah" waterfall await. Direct any questions to the information center inside the Multnomah Falls Lodge (below). *I-84 exit 31.* ☎ *503/695-2372. Daily dawn–dusk; information center daily 9am–5pm. Free admission.*

Recharge with a bite at the historic **❺ Multnomah Falls Lodge** at the base of the falls, built in 1925. Look for an outdoor table in the summer. The historic structure was threatened by the Eagle Creek fire in 2017 but escaped destruction. *All meals daily.* ☎ *503/695-2376. www. multnomahfallslodge.com. $$.*

❻ ★★★ kids Triple waterfall hike. With 77 cascades on the Oregon side of the Gorge (in case you were wondering, that's Washington on the other side), picking which ones to visit can be tough. A relatively easy 4-mile loop trail hits no fewer than three, including an optional fourth, all without climbing over 800 feet. Start at the Horsetail Falls Trailhead on the Columbia River Highway. After ogling 176-foot **Horsetail Falls,** take Trail #400 up a mossy slope to reach 80-foot **Ponytail Falls,** which have undercut the hillside so much that the trail leads behind them. From here you'll climb a bit farther to cross a bridge over the upper end of narrow Oneonta Gorge, before reaching a side trail (#438) that climbs almost a mile to **Triple Falls,** spilling over 100 feet into a large pool. Come back down to Trail #400 and take a left to descend to the Oneonta Gorge Trailhead. From here you can walk east along the highway half a mile back to your car—or else, if you're properly outfitted with waterproof waders, and limber enough to climb over slippery fallen logs, take the stairs down into cool, deep Oneonta Gorge and wade upstream 1,000 feet to **Oneonta Falls.** *Horsetail Falls Trailhead on the Columbia River Highway, 1½ miles east of I-84 exit 35.*

7 ★ **kids Bonneville Lock and Dam.** Completed in 1936 for hydropower and river navigation, this massive dam stretches 3,460 feet across the Columbia. Four sections connect both banks and three islands, one of which holds the **Bradford Island Visitors Center,** where you can watch through underwater windows as native salmon migrate upstream from October through December. (Fish ladders were added later.) The California sea lions that congregate at the base of the dam gobble so many fish that wildlife officials sometimes have to relocate them. Next to the dam, the **Bonneville Fish Hatchery** (☎ 541-374-8393) raises Chinook, Coho, and steelhead salmon and has display ponds where you can feed rainbow trout and white sturgeon. (Don't miss 10-foot-long Herman the Sturgeon, who's over 60 years old.) *I-84 exit 40.* ☎ *541/374-8820. www.nwp. usace.army.mil/locations. Visitor center daily 9am–5pm; fish hatchery daily 7:30am–dusk. Free admission.*

8 ★ **Cascade Locks.** A series of rapids kept steamboats from ascending the Columbia past this point until a series of locks were blasted from solid stone in 1896. Forty-two years later, most of them have disappeared beneath the rising waters of Lake Bonneville, behind Bonneville Dam. The upper locks are still above water, though, and are part of **Cascade Locks Marine Park,** with a small museum on river history and the Oregon Pony, the first steam engine in the West. It's the home base of the **Columbia Gorge Sternwheeler** (☎ 503/224-3900 or 800/224-3901; www.sternwheeler.com), a three-deck paddle-wheeler that gives tours of the gorge. You can cross to Washington on the **Bridge of the Gods** ($2 toll) named after a natural bridge that once stood here according to Native American legend. It's open to cars and foot traffic, including hikers on the Pacific Crest Trail. *I-84 exit 44.* ☎ *541/374-8484. www.cascadelocks.net. Museum May–Sept Tues–Sun 2–5pm. Admission $3 adults, $2 seniors/youth, $5 family.*

9 ★★ **Hood River.** The "Aspen of windsurfing" owes its worldwide reputation to the regular winds that rush down the gorge, sometimes topping 30mph in the summer. In fact, Hood River is an all-around adventure-sports hotspot, with kayaking, mountain biking, and hiking galore in the gorge and the nearby slopes of Mt. Hood. At night and on the rare calm day, there are plenty of shops and eateries to explore.

Fish ladder at Bonneville Dam.

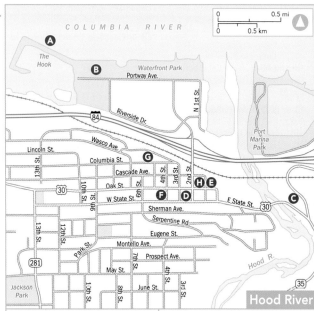

COLUMBIA RIVER

Hood River

You can watch windsurfers and kite-boarders leap whitecaps from **A The Hook,** a short protected harbor, and the adjacent **B Water-front Park,** both on the opposite (river) side of I-84 from town. If you're inspired to give either a try, stop by **C Windance Sailboards** (108 Hwy. 35 at Hwy. 30; ☎ 541/386-2131; www.windance.com) for rentals and lessons. (Keep in mind that learning here is like learning to drive in Manhattan: difficult, but then you're ready for anything.) To take on one of the many mountain-bike trails on the flanks of Mt. Hood to the south, head to **D Discover Bicycles** (210 State St.; ☎ 541/386-4820; www.discoverbicycles.com) for tips and the largest rental

selection in the Northwest. The bulk of the town's restaurants are on or near Oak Street (U.S. 30), including **E Celilo Restaurant and Bar** (16 Oak St.; ☎ 541/386-5710; www.celilorestaurant.com) and **F Kaze Japanese Restaurant** (212 4th St.; ☎ 541/387-0434). One notable exception is the **G Full Sail Tasting Room & Pub** (506 Columbia St.; ☎ 541/386-2247; www.fullsailbrewing.com), one of Oregon's first and most famous craft breweries. If all this makes you want to spend the night, the 100-year-old **H Hood River Hotel** (102 Oak St.; ☎ 800/386-1859; www.hoodriverhotel.com) is the city's oldest and one of its best.

⑩ ★★ kids Hood River Valley Fruit Loop. The river valley between the Columbia and Mt. Hood packs a lot into a small and scenic area: wineries, beehives, lavender farms, and 2.4 million fruit trees, almost a quarter of Oregon's total. (It's the country's top

Mount Hood Railroad

Experience a bit of time travel aboard a 1906-era railroad through the Hood River Valley. Started as a freight line, it still pulls the occasional freight car but is mostly used for scenic tours to Odell (2 hr. round-trip) and Parkdale (4 hr. round-trip). It's worth it to splurge for a seat in the upper dome car, and pack a lunch for the short stopovers. Along the way, you'll get views of Mt. Hood and the gorge, and experience one of the few switchback tracks still in use in the U.S. Special tours throughout the year range from brunch and Murder Mystery dinner trains to Western Robbery rides and a holiday Polar Express. ☎ *800/872-4661. www.mthoodrr. com. Trains run year-round Tues–Sun, schedule varies, regular excursions $35–$55 adults, $30–$50 children, meal trains and special excursions $30–$82 per person.*

pear-growing district.) A 35-mile loop drive along Hwy. 281 and Hwy. 35, through the burgs of Dee, Odell, Oak Grove, Pine Grove, and Mount Hood, is a wonderful way to spend a day meandering from one farm, roadside produce stand, and alpaca ranch to another. Festivals from spring through fall celebrate what's in season, from cherries in July to pumpkins in November. *Maps & information at Hood River visitor center, I-84 exit 64.* ☎ *541/386-2000 or 800/366-3530. www.hoodriverfruitloop.com. Fruit tree blossoms peak in Apr; fruit stands (cherries, pears, plums, apples, pumpkins) July–Oct; fall foliage in Oct.*

⓫ ★ **The Dalles.** The eastern end of the Columbia River Highway is a historic city at one of the few spots along the river where early traders could load boats and Oregon Trail pioneers could raft their way to Oregon City, the end of the trail. It's full of 19th-century buildings and more recent murals. History buffs can learn more about the significance of The Dales at the small but intriguing **Fort Dalles Museum,** which occupies the surgeon's quarters of the 1856 fort. *500 W. 15th St.* ☎ *541/296-4547. www.fortdallesmuseum.org. Admission $5 adults, $4 seniors, $1 children. Mar–Oct daily 10am–5pm; Nov–Apr Fri–Sun 10am–5pm.*

⓬ ★★ **Columbia Gorge Discovery Center and Museum.** Everything you ever wanted to know about the gorge, from the Ice Age and Lewis and Clark through the finer points of how to windsurf, comes together in this exceptional museum. The wide-windowed building itself is a wonder, and its collection spans geology, natural history, and 12,000 years of human habitation, with films, photos, and artifacts. Living history exhibits and a live raptor program round out the experience. Outside, a paved trail connects wetlands, a pond, and viewpoints of the gorge, and continues 4.5 miles to the Dalles. *5000 Discovery Dr.* ☎ *541/296-8600. www.gorgediscovery.org. Daily 9am–5pm. Admission $9 adults, $7 seniors, $5 children 6–16, free for kids 6 & under.*

Willamette Valley Wine Tour

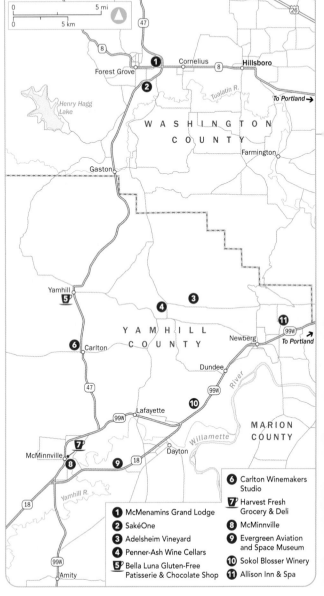

1 McMenamins Grand Lodge
2 SakéOne
3 Adelsheim Vineyard
4 Penner-Ash Wine Cellars
5 Bella Luna Gluten-Free Patisserie & Chocolate Shop
6 Carlton Winemakers Studio
7 Harvest Fresh Grocery & Deli
8 McMinnville
9 Evergreen Aviation and Space Museum
10 Sokol Blosser Winery
11 Allison Inn & Spa

The fertile, sheltered valley of the Willamette ("wih-LAM-it") River, the "promised land" for so many settlers on the Oregon Trail, is now one of the country's top winegrowing regions. It's a kind of anti-Napa, with little of the pretentiousness or crowds, although summer weekends can get very busy. Pinot noir is gospel here, but you'll find other cool-weather vintages as well, including pinot gris, Rieslings, Gewürztraminers, and ever-improving chardonnays. You'll also find roadside produce stands and farms growing everything from tulips to hazelnuts. (*Be warned:* Hwy. 99W can get choked with traffic on weekends, so consider an alternate route.) START: **U.S. 26 west to OR 47, about 27 miles from Portland to Forest Grove.**

1 ★ McMenamins Grand Lodge. One of the, well, grandest properties in the McMenamins portfolio, this 1922 retirement home is full of all the kaleidoscopic artwork, comfy lounges, and craft beer you'd expect, along with a wine bar, spa, movie theater, soaking pool, and four on-site choices for food and libations. There's even a disc golf course on the expansive lawns that surround the property. The less expensive guestrooms have shared bathrooms. *3505 Pacific Ave., Forest Grove. ☎ 877/922-9533 or 503/992-9533. www.mcmenamins.com/GrandLodge. Doubles $75–$210.*

2 ★ SakéOne. Leave it to Oregon to have the only American-owned craft sake brewery in the world. After a tour of the facilities, head to the tasting room to sample their popular blue-bottled Momokawa line, as well as the fruit-infused Moonstone and undiluted "G" brands. *820 Elm St. off OR 47, Forest Grove. ☎ 800/550-SAKE (7253) or 503/357-7056. www.sakeone.com. Tasting room daily 11am–5pm; tasting flights $5–$15 per person.*

3 ★ Adelsheim Vineyard. One of Oregon's most popular pinot noir producers, Adelsheim has a big tasting room and a patio overlooking the vineyard. Tastings aren't cheap, but you can sample vintages that aren't on the market—including some outstanding single-vineyard wines—and the fee goes toward purchases. *16800 NE Calkins Lane, Newberg. ☎ 503/538-3652. www.adelsheim.com. Tasting room daily 11am–4pm. Fee $15. Tour by appointment only.*

4 ★★★ Penner-Ash Wine Cellars. It's a bit tricky to find, but winemaker Lynn Penner-Ash's

Autumn at a Willamette Valley vineyard.

Guided Wine Tours

If you can't tell a pinot noir from a petite Syrah—or if you just don't want to have to pick a designated driver—try an in-depth guided tour of Willamette wine country. On most Saturdays from March through December, **Grape Escape** (☎ 503/283-3380; www.grape escapetours.com) runs outings with highly trained guides that include pick-up and drop-off, food and tasting at three wineries in a day ($95-$125 for half-day tour). **Oregon Wine Tours** (☎ 503/681-WINE [9463]; www.orwinetours.com) does the same, with themed excursions such as small producers and "ABP" ("Anything But Pinot"). Their all-day tours start at $375 per person for one or two people).

winery offers outstanding vintages and wonderful views from a hilltop between Yamhill and Newberg. The pinot noirs and Syrahs are deservedly famous, but they also make viogniers, rubeos, Rieslings, and rosés. *15771 NE Ribbon Ridge Rd., Newberg. ☎ 503/554-5545. www. pennerash.com. Tasting room daily 11am–5pm. Fees $25–$50. Tour by appointment only.*

Anyone who's on a gluten-free diet will be happy to stop in at **5️⃣ Bella Luna Gluten-Free Patisserie & Chocolate Shop** for a gluten-free sweet. *185 S. Maple St., Yamhill, OR. ☎ 503/662-0098. www.bella lunapatisserie.com. $.*

6️⃣ ★★ Carlton Winemakers Studio. Eleven vintners banded together here under one roof offer tastings of up to 40 different wines. If you're pressed for time or just like to sample a wide range, it's a good choice to visit. The modern building was the first in the country to be certified by the U.S. Green Building Council. *801 N. Scott St., Carlton. ☎ 503/852-6100. www. winemakersstudio.com. Tasting room daily 11am–5pm. Fee $10–$25.*

Stock up for your winery picnic lunch at **7️⃣ Harvest Fresh Grocery & Deli**, a natural food store offering local produce, sandwiches, salads, and fresh-squeezed juices and smoothies. *251 NE 3rd St., McMinnville. ☎ 503/472-5740. www.harvestfresh.com. $.*

8️⃣ ★★ McMinnville. Amble down 3rd Street, "Oregon's Favorite Main Street," to find local shops, boutiques, wine-tasting rooms, and top-notch restaurants. *Bon Appétit* magazine dubbed McMinnville one of the country's best small towns for food lovers, and you can see why at places like **Thistle** (228 NE Evans St.; ☎ 503/472-9623; www.thistlerestaurant. com) and **Bistro Maison** (729 NE 3rd St.; ☎ 503/474-1888; www.bistromaison.com). For a flavorful and filling breakfast, brunch or lunch, try **Crescent Café** (526 NE 3rd St.; ☎ 503/435-2655; www.crescentcafeonthird.com). The rooftop bar and deck at the **McMenamins Hotel Oregon** (310 NE Evans St.; ☎ 888/472-8427 or 503/472-8427; www.mcmenamins.com/Hotel Oregon) is a perfect stop at the

Oregon winemakers share a tasting room at Carlton Winemakers Studio.

end of a wine tour day. (The tater tots are a guilty pleasure.)

⑨ ★★★ kids Evergreen Aviation and Space Museum. In between bites of brie and sips of Syrah, how about a side trip to see the largest plane ever built? Howard Hughes's "Spruce Goose," a wooden flying boat with a 320-foot wingspan, flew exactly once, for 1 minute, before ending up at this hangarlike museum alongside fighter jets, stunt planes, a Mercury space capsule, and much more. There's also an IMAX theater and the **Wings & Waves Waterpark** (www.wingsandwaveswaterpark. com) with a wave pool and ten waterslides—including four that start from inside a real 747 plopped on the roof. *500 NE Capt. Michael King Smith Way, McMinnville.* ☎ *503/434-4185. www.evergreenmuseum.org. Museum admission $27 adults, $24 seniors, $19 children 5–16. Waterpark admission $29, or $20 if under 42 inches tall. Museum daily 9am–5pm; waterpark summer daily 10am–8pm (check website for off-season hours).*

⑩ ★★★ Sokol Blosser Winery. Whites are the favorites at this popular Dundee winery, the first in the country to receive LEED certification for sustainable practices. Tour the vineyards in a custom biodiesel ATV to see organic farming techniques and a 24kW solar array in action. *5000 Sokol Blosser Lane, Dundee.* ☎ *800/582-6668 or 503/864-2282. www.sokolblosser. com. Tasting room daily 10am–4pm. Fee $15–$25. Tours by appointment only.*

⑪ ★★★ Allison Inn & Spa. The only high-end getaway in Wine Country makes an excellent base for wine touring. Rooms are huge, with terraces or balconies, hot tubs, and the lush grounds are perfect for strolling and sipping your latest purchase. Relax in the spa and enjoy excellent wine-country cuisine at the Jory restaurant. What really earns raves, though, is the attentive but unobtrusive service. *2525 Allison Lane, Newberg.* ☎ *503/554-2525. www.theallison.com. Rooms $350–$450.*

Oregon Coast

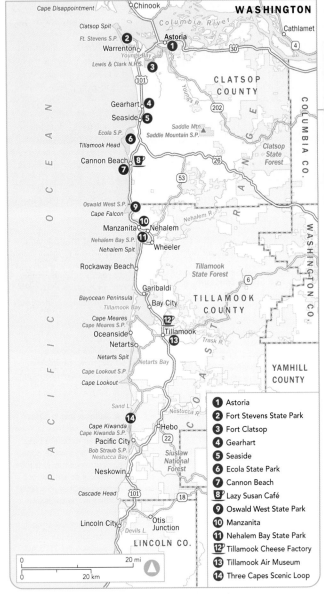

1 Astoria
2 Fort Stevens State Park
3 Fort Clatsop
4 Gearhart
5 Seaside
6 Ecola State Park
7 Cannon Beach
8 Lazy Susan Café
9 Oswald West State Park
10 Manzanita
11 Nehalem Bay State Park
12 Tillamook Cheese Factory
13 Tillamook Air Museum
14 Three Capes Scenic Loop

The northern part of Oregon's coastline gets the most visitors, and it's easy to see why: The thickly forested Coast Range mountains meet the crashing waves of the Pacific in towering headlands and wide, flat, white-sand beaches punctuated by enormous, offshore rock monoliths. Yes, it's too cold and dangerous to swim (even with a wet suit) but summers are uncrowded by California or East Coast standards, and winter brings its own stormy beauty—plus migrating gray whales. And thanks to a forward-thinking 1967 law, all of Oregon's breathtaking coastline is forever public. START: U.S. 30 West from Portland, 100 miles.

❶ ★★★ Astoria. The oldest American settlement west of the Mississippi was founded as Fort Astoria in 1811 by fur trappers working for John Jacob Astor, America's first multimillionaire. After years of neglect, and now that cruise ships stop here in the summer, Astoria is undergoing an exciting renaissance. Restored Victorian homes grace the hillsides, and good restaurants, microbreweries, coffee shops, art galleries, and shops are revitalizing the downtown. Spend an afternoon strolling the riverwalk, watching massive cargo ships and barges pass and sea lions lounge on piers. While you're there, enjoy local seafood-with-a-view at

Astoria Column tops Coxcomb Hill.

BRIDGEwater Bistro (20 Basin St.; ☎ 503/325-6777; www.bridgewaterbistro.com) or the more casual **Clemente's Café & Public House** (175 14th St.; ☎ **503/325-1067**). Climb the staircase inside the historic, 125-foot-high **Astoria Column** atop Coxcomb Hill (www.astoriacolumn.org; daily dawn–dusk) for a panoramic view of the town and the mighty river. The 1885 Queen Anne-style **Flavel House** (441 Eighth St.; ☎ 503/325-2203; www.cumtux.org; daily 10am–4pm) provides a fascinating glimpse into the life of a wealthy Astorian sea captain and family in the late 19th century. Don't miss the outstanding **Columbia River Maritime Museum** (1792 Marine Dr.; ☎ 503/325-2323; www.crmm.org; daily 9:30am–5pm), with exhibits on the history of the country's second-largest river and the wreck-strewn "Graveyard of the Pacific" at its mouth. If you're inspired to stay, the **Cannery Pier Hotel** (10 Basin St.; ☎ 888/325-4996 or 503/325-4996; www.cannerypierhotel.com) is a modern luxury hotel built on an old cannery pier stretching 600 feet out in the river. *www.astoriaoregon.com.*

❷ ★ Fort Stevens State Park. This 4,200-acre park in Oregon's far northwestern corner is guarded by a fort built during the Civil War to protect the mouth of the Columbia River. It was the only military

The wreck of the Peter Iredale in Fort Stevens State Park.

installation in the continental U.S. to be fired on by the Japanese during World War II—17 shells in June 1942, to be exact. Now it consists of a military museum surrounded by huge concrete bunkers and paths for hiking and bicycling. There's also a lake for swimming and a large campground with yurts and cabins. Head to the park's Pacific beach to find the rusted wreck of the **Peter Iredale,** a four-masted steel sailboat that ran ashore on October 25, 1906. Living history events happen from April to September, including a Civil War reenactment over Labor Day weekend. *8 miles from Astoria via U.S. 101 & Ridge Rd.* ☎ *503/861-1671 or 800/551-6949. www.oregonstate parks.org/park_179.php. Museum summer & fall daily 10am–6pm; winter & spring daily 10am–4pm. Admission $5 per car. Campsites $22–$56; cabins $100.*

❸ ★★★ kids **Fort Clatsop—Lewis and Clark National Historic Park.** After slogging across half of North America, Lewis and Clark spent the cold, rainy winter of 1805–06 holed up in a log stockade they built near present-day Astoria. Named after the friendly local Clatsop Indians, the reconstructed fort is part of the Lewis and Clark National and State Historical Parks group. The primitive buildings give

an accurate and atmospheric picture of the conditions at the fort over 200 years ago. In the summer, costumed interpreters demonstrate frontier-era skills such as making candles and shooting a flintlock rifle. From here the 6.5-mile **Fort to Sea Trail** leads through forest, dunes, and fields to **Sunset Beach State Recreation Area.** *Off U.S. 101, 5 miles southwest of Astoria.* ☎ *503/861-2471. www.nps.gov/ lewi. Admission $3 adults, free for ages 16 & under. Mid-June to Labor Day daily 9am–6pm; Labor Day to mid-June daily 9am–5pm.*

❹ ★ **Gearhart.** If your goal is to get away from it all, even by Oregon Coast standards, then this tiny beach town is for you. Beyond a scant handful of tourist-oriented businesses, Gearhart is just private homes—expensive ones—and a nearly deserted 4-mile stretch of beach. At the **Gearhart Ocean Inn** (67 N. Cottage Ave.; ☎ 503/738-7373; www.gearhartoceaninn.com), you can steam your own clams in the kitchenettes or walk across the street to the cozy **Pacific Way Bakery & Café** (601 Pacific Way; ☎ 503/738-0245) for a croissant or Dungeness crab ravioli. The adjacent bakery (open Thurs-Sun) is a great place for scones, muffins, and sweet treats. Head to the end of Wellington Street at the south end

Exploring the dunes along the Oregon coast.

of town to find a short, unmarked trail to the **Necanicum River estuary,** often packed with shore birds stalking the mudflats for dinner. From here, the Pacific dunes are just a short walk west.

5 ★ **kids Seaside.** Oregon's version of the Atlantic City (without the gambling) brings a bit of tacky fun to the otherwise staid beach towns around here, with a string of souvenir shops, video arcades, minigolf courses, and amusement-park rides. The town itself is full of historic cottages dating to the turn of the 20th century, but what draws most visitors is the wide white-sand beach and the 2-mile beachfront **promenade**, unique in Oregon. Lifeguards are on duty throughout the summer, making this a popular beach with families. There are plenty of places to buy kites or rent three- and four-wheeled beach cycles. At the **Seaside Aquarium** (200 N. Promenade; ☎ 503/738-6211; www.seasideaquarium.com), one of the oldest on the West Coast, you can touch a sea anemone or feed a seal. *80 miles from Portland via U.S. 26. www.seasideor. com.*

6 ★★★ **Ecola State Park.** Lewis and Clark arrived here in

The beach at Ecola State Park.

1806—the farthest south they ventured on the Oregon coast—to buy whale blubber and see a whale washed up on the beach. Their 16-year-old Indian guide, Sacagawea, was in the scouting party. You can trace part of their route on a 2.5-mile loop trail through steep forests of Sitka spruce, or take a slightly longer trail 600 feet up to the top of Tillamook Head, which Clark called "the steepest worst & highest mountain I ever ascended." (It's not that bad, and the views of the coastline are more than worth it.) More hiking trails lead to the beach, a primitive hike-in campsite, and picnic areas on high bluffs, perfect for spotting whales in the winter and spring. *Just north of Cannon Beach on U.S. 101.* ☎ *800/551-6949 or 503/436-2844. www.oregonstateparks.org/park_188.php. Fee $5 per vehicle.*

7 ★★★ **Cannon Beach.** Named for a cannon that washed ashore from a shipwreck in 1846, Cannon Beach is the most upscale and charming (if highly commercialized) town on the North Coast, full of cedar-shingled homes, art galleries, shops, and good restaurants and hotels. Iconic **Haystack Rock** is a 235-foot-high sea stack (formed by wave erosion) just off the wide and windy beach, home to sea birds like tufted puffins and surrounded by tide pools. Follow up an intimate seafood dinner at **Newmans at 988** (988 S. Hemlock St.; ☎ 503/436-1151; www.newmansat988.com) with a night at the **Stephanie Inn** (2740 S. Pacific St.; ☎ 800/633-3466 or 503/436-2221; www.stephanie-inn.com), regularly listed among the most romantic in Oregon. The **Inn at Cannon Beach** (3215 S. Hemlock St.; ☎ 800/321-6304; www.atcannonbeach.com) is off the main drag but near the

beach, with oceanfront balcony rooms overlooking Haystack Rock. *80 miles from Portland via U.S. 26. www.cannonbeach.org.*

Enjoy a marionberry scone at **8** **Lazy Susan Café.** This two-story Cannon Beach cottage is one of the best breakfast spots in town. They're also open for lunch and dinner, with salads, sandwiches, and seafood stews. *126 N. Hemlock St.* ☎ *503/436-2816. www.lazy-susan-café.com. $.*

9 ★★ **Oswald West State Park.** Mountains meet the sea in a show-stopping way at this coastal park. A 15-minute hike to the secluded, crescent-shaped beach keeps out most of the crowds. More trails lead to viewpoints from the headlands on either side, and the Oregon Coast Trail goes up and over 1,600-foot **Neahkahnie Mountain.** Translated as "place of the supreme deity" in the native Tillamook language, the mountain is reputed to hide a lost Spanish fortune that has cost more than one treasure-hunter's life. One trailhead is just south of the park boundary on U.S. 101. From there, it's 2 steep miles through dense forest to the summit. *10 miles south of Cannon Beach.* ☎ *800/551-6949. www.oregonstateparks.org/park_195.php. Fee $5 per vehicle.*

10 ★★★ **Manzanita.** A favorite getaway on the North Coast, this 600-person village has one main street and not much to do besides eat, sleep, and go to the beach. It's close enough to Cannon Beach and numerous state parks to enjoy those by day, but all you can hear at night are the waves. The **Ocean Inn at Manzanita** (32 Laneda Ave.; ☎ 866/368-7701 or 503/368-7701;

Strolling on the beach at Manzanita.

www.oceaninnatmanzanita.com) has 10 condo and kitchenette units right on the sand, and the **Coast Cabins** (635 Laneda Ave.; ☎ 800/435-1269 or 503/368-7113; www.coastcabins.com) are five cedar cottages with a Japan-meets-Scandinavia aesthetic. The **Bread and Ocean Bakery** (154 Laneda Ave.; ☎ 503/368-5823) is one of the better lunch and dinner places in town, with great cinnamon rolls and sandwiches. *14½ miles south of Cannon Beach on U.S. 101. www.explore manzanita.com.*

⓫ ★ Nehalem Bay State Park. This park covers most of the sandy spit separating Nehalem Bay and the mouth of the Nehalem River from the ocean. You'll find a campground, rental yurts, and paths for horses, bikes, and joggers. In summer, guided horseback rides are available for anywhere from 1 hour to all day. Or go crabbing, fishing, or sailing around the calm waters of the bay, paddle a sea kayak upriver, or head offshore for surfing or windsurfing. Some parts of the beach may be closed to protect nesting seabirds. *☎ 503/368-5154 or 800/551-6949. www.oregonstateparks.org/ park_201.php. Fee $5 per car; yurts $54–$64; horseback rides $75–$150 per person for 1–2 hr., full day $400.*

After a tour of **⓬ Tillamook Cheese Factory,** which produces 167,000 pounds of cheese every day, you can sample the goods at the attached store, including cheese curds (aka "squeaky cheese"), ice cream, and fudge. *4175 Hwy. 101 N. ☎ 800/542-7290 or 503/815-1300. www.tillamook. com/cheese-factory. $.*

⓭ ★ kids Tillamook Air Museum. More than 30 restored vintage planes and helicopters have found a home in a former World War II Navy blimp hangar that stands over 15 stories high. The collection includes a P-38 Lightning, a P51-Mustang, and a Bf-109 Messerschmitt. *6030 Hangar*

The Cape Meares Lighthouse.

Rd. ☎ 503/842-1130. www.tillamook air.com. *Admission $9.75 adults, $8.75 seniors, $6.50 youth 5–17. Tues–Sun 9am–5pm.*

⓮ ★★★ Three Capes Scenic Loop. Perhaps the prettiest drive on this part of the coast, this 30-mile scenic byway takes you from Tillamook to Pacific City, past view after view of the rugged coast. Take 3rd Street out of Tillamook toward the ocean and turn right on Bayocean Road to reach **Cape Meares State Scenic Viewpoint,** home to Oregon's largest Sitka spruce and the **Cape Meares Lighthouse** (☎ 503/842-2244; www.capemeareslighthouse.org). The 200-foot-high headland is the only place in the U.S. where you can see three National Wildlife

Refuges at once: Cape Mears, Oregon Islands, and Three Arch Rocks. Look for peregrine falcons and gray whales in the winter. Keep going to **Cape Lookout State Park** (☎ 503/842-4981 or 800/551-6949; www.oregonstateparks.org/park_186.php), where a 2.5-mile trail winds through dense old-growth rainforest to the tip of the peninsula, a great place to spot gray whales. There's also a campground (sites $25-$56) with yurts ($54–$64), cabins ($100) and a $5 entry fee per car. Past Oceanside and Netarts Bay, **Cape Kiwanda State Natural Area** (☎ 800/551-6949; www.oregonstateparks.org/park_180.php) has giant sand dune popular with hang gliders. Another giant sea stack looms offshore. ●

The Savvy Traveler

Before You Go

Tourist Offices

The **Travel Portland Visitor Information Center** in Pioneer Courthouse Square downtown (701 SW 6th Ave.; ☎ 503/275-8355 or 877/678-5263; www.travelportland. com) is open Monday through Friday 8:30am to 5:30pm, Saturday 10am to 4pm, and Sunday 10am to 2pm from May through October. For destinations outside the city, contact the **Oregon Tourism Commission**, 670 Hawthorne St. SE, Suite 240, Salem, OR 97301 (☎ 800/547-7842; www.travel oregon.com).

The Best Times to Go

Summer—defined locally as beginning on July 5, when the clouds generally retreat—is gorgeous in Portland. Sunshine replaces drizzle, lawns go from deep green to dry brown, and temperatures are warm, but usually not uncomfortably so. (That said, there have been temperature spikes into the 100s in recent years.) From June through September, it's highly advisable to book hotel and car reservations ahead of time—as far ahead as possible for weekends, holidays, and events like the Rose Festival. Spring and fall are more of a crapshoot, weather-wise, but you might hit a week or even two of sunshine, and gardens in Portland are at their lushest. Prices fall and reservations open up in these seasons, and even more so in the winter, except for the holidays. Winters are generally mild but gray and wet, and a few days of snow is not uncommon. But the snow, of course, is what skiers want when they head to nearby Mt. Hood.

Previous page: Biking in Portland.

Festivals & Special Events

SPRING April brings the **Spring Beer & Wine Fest** (www.spring beerfest.com), filling the Convention Center with craft microbrews, regional wines, spirits, food, crafts, and music. This is also the month to catch the **Tulip Festival** at Wooden Shoe Tulip Farm in Woodburn (☎ 503/634-2243 or 800/711-2006; www.woodenshoe.com), whose fields of vibrant blooms will make you feel as if you're in Holland, not 35 miles south of Portland.

May starts with the **Cinco de Mayo Fiesta** (www.cincodemayo. org), supposedly the country's largest, which celebrates Portland's sister-city status with Guadalajara, Mexico. Food, entertainment, and music are all on the bill in Governor Tom McCall Waterfront Park. At the end of the month, the **Mother's Day Rhododendron Show** at Crystal Springs Rhododendron Garden, SE 28th Avenue and Woodstock Boulevard (☎ 503/771-8386), is a riot of blossoming rhododendrons and azaleas.

SUMMER June is the month of extended events, led by the **Portland Rose Festival** (☎ 503/227-2681; www.rosefestival.org), the city's oldest, biggest, and most famous celebration. Three weeks of events include the **Rose Festival Grand Floral Parade,** a starlight parade, the election of the Rose Queen, a waterfront carnival, and dragon boat races on the river.

June also brings the month-long **Pedalpalooza** (www.shift2bikes. org/pedalpalooza), an only-in-Portland festival of all things bike-related. Hundreds of events are held, most of them free, including the immense **World Naked Bike Ride**—we're talking thousands of bicyclists in the buff. The **Portland Pride Festival and Parade** (www.pridenw.org) happens over a weekend in mid-June, with a Pride Parade on Sunday, live entertainment, a drag race (heels, not wheels), and a pet parade.

Over the extended Fourth of July weekend, the **Waterfront Blues Festival** (☎ 503/282-0555; www.waterfrontbluesfest.com) fills Governor Tom McCall Waterfront Park with 4 days of national headliners. I it's the largest blues festival west of the Mississippi.

The last full weekend in July brings more beer, this time in the form of the 4-day **Oregon Brewers Festival** (☎ 503/778-5917; www.oregonbrewfest.com), one of the largest and oldest craft-beer festivals in the U.S. Waterfront Park is the setting for close to 100 craft brewers from home and abroad, with demonstrations, exhibits, food, and live music.

In late July, indie music fans flock to **PDX Pop Now!** (www.pdxpopnow.com), a free, all-ages festival of local music featuring upwards of 50 artists selected by public vote. When the 3-day event is over, you can take home a two-CD compilation.

Mid-August's **The Bite of Oregon** (www.biteoforegon.com), a fundraiser for Special Olympics Oregon, features food and wine samples from local chefs and regional wineries, along with live music, cooking demos, and other entertainment.

Summer also brings many local street fairs on the east side of the city, mostly 1-day affairs with food and drink vendors, music, crafts, and the occasional bouncy castle.

FALL In early September, **Musicfest NW** (www.musicfestnw.com) fills Waterfront Park and the clubs of Portland with local musicians and national acts for 4 days. The **Time-Based Art Festival** (☎ 503/242-1419; www.pica.org/tba) consists of 10 days of modern visual and performance arts sponsored by the Portland Institute for Contemporary Arts.

In mid-November, the **Northwest Film & Video Festival** (☎ 503/221-1156; www.nwfilm.org/festivals) brings a host of short films, documentaries, and features by independent filmmakers from the Pacific Northwest.

WINTER Get in the holiday mood with the **ZooLights Festival** (www.oregonzoo.org), which includes music, kids' activities, and a special holiday train.

The **Portland International Film Festival** (☎ 503/228-7433; www.nwfilm.org) in February brings 100 films from all over the world to theaters around the city. This same month, the Oregon Convention Center becomes one huge bistro during the **Oregon Seafood and Wine Festival** (www.pdxseafoodandwinefestival.com), which happily coincides with the Dungeness crab season.

The Weather

Ah yes, the weather. If this almost suspiciously appealing city has a catch, it's what goes on outside from about November to May: days of gray skies and mist, light rain, or downright downpours interspersed with mild, sunny days. Hotel rates are lower in Portland and along the coast. Bring rain gear and a jacket or fleece. (Nothing brands you as a tourist like using an umbrella.) Temperatures regularly drop into the low 40s in the heart of winter, when the Cascades are being buried in snow.

But, as locals are quick to remind you, the summers are wonderful, even if they don't reliably start, weather-wise, until the 5th of July. Then you can usually count on 3 months of near-constant sunshine with hardly a drop of precipitation for weeks on end. Temperatures seldom climb above the low 90s, although summer temps have spiked into the low-100s and stayed there for 3 or 4 days in recent years. This is when hotel and car reservations become essential, especially on the weekends and *especially* on the coast.

Spring and fall are more of a gamble, with occasional windows of sunny weather lasting for a few days or even a few weeks. Even then it's a good idea to have an extra layer ready, ideally one that's waterproof.

With climate change upon us, it's a bit specious to provide a month-by-month weather summary based on past weather data because Portland is now seeing spikes in temperature in all seasons. But the following chart provides a general idea.

Useful Websites

- **www.oregonian.com** is the website for the daily *Oregonian* newspaper.

- **www.wweek.com** takes you to the *Willamette Week* weekly newspaper site.

- **www.portlandmercury.com** is the website of the *Portland Mercury,* another popular weekly.

- **www.travelportland.com** is for the Portland Visitor's Association.

- **www.pdxpipeline.com** offers music, art, and entertainment listings.

- **www.pdxkparent.com** is the place to go for children's events and activities.

- **www.opentable.com** offers information about and reservations for Portland eateries.

Car Rentals

All major car-rental companies have desks at the airport, which is the most convenient place to pick up a car. Across from the baggage-claim area you'll find Alamo, Avis, Budget, Dollar, Enterprise, Hertz, National, and Thrifty. It's a good idea to comparison shop before you book. Rates drop in the rainy months.

If you're visiting from abroad and plan to rent a car in the U.S., keep in mind that foreign driver's licenses are usually recognized in the U.S., but you may want to consider obtaining an international driver's license.

Getting **There**

By Plane
Portland International Airport
(PDX; ☎ 877/739-4636 or 503/460-4234; www.flypdx.com), located 10 miles northeast of downtown along the Columbia River, is an astonishingly pleasant and efficient airport. You can get maps and brochures from the information booth by the baggage-claim area. Some hotels have courtesy shuttle service to and from the airport, especially the ones nearby; be sure to ask when you make a reservation. Carriers flying to PDX include:

- **Air Canada** (☎ 888/247-2262; www.aircanada.ca)

- **Alaska Airlines** (☎ 800/252-7522; www.alaskaair.com)

- **American Airlines** (☎ 800/433-7300; www.aa.com)

- **Condor Air** ☎ 866-960-7915; www.condorair.com)

- **Delta** (☎ 800/221-1212; www.delta.com)

- **Frontier** (☎ 800/432-1359; www.flyfrontier.com)

PORTLAND'S AVERAGE MONTHLY TEMPERATURES & RAINFALL

NEW YORK'S AVERAGE TEMPERATURE & RAINFALL

	JAN	FEB	MAR	APR	MAY	JUNE
Temp. (°F)	40	43	46	50	57	63
Temp. (°C)	4	6	8	10	14	17
Days of Rain	18	16	17	14	12	10

	JULY	AUG	SEPT	OCT	NOV	DEC
Temp. (°F)	68	67	63	54	46	41
Temp. (°C)	20	19	17	12	8	5
Days of Rain	4	5	8	13	18	19

- **Hawaiian Air** (☎ 800-367-5320; www.hawaiianair.com)

- **Horizon Air** (☎ 800/547-9308; www.horizonair.com)

- **JetBlue** (☎ 800/538-2583; www.jetblue.com)

- **Seaport Air** (☎ 888-573-2767; www.seaportair.com)

- **Southwest** (☎ 800/435-9792; www.southwest.com)

- **Spirit Air** (☎ 800/772-7117; www.spirit.com)

- **United** (☎ 800/864-8331; www.united.com)

- **Virgin America** (☎ 877/359-8474; www.virginamerica.com)

To get downtown by car, follow the signs to downtown via I-205 and I-84 west, and then cross the Willamette River using the Morrison Bridge exit. Without traffic, the trip takes about 20 minutes.

Taxis wait outside baggage claim; a ride downtown costs between $40 and $45. It is also legal to call **Uber** (www.uber.com) or **Lyft** (www.lyft.com) from the airport. **Blue Star** ☎ 503/249-1837; www.bluestarbus.com) runs a shared shuttle bus to the airport for $14 per person each way to and from downtown.

The easiest and least expensive way to get into the city from the airport is by **MAX light-rail.** Trains leave the airport station on the lower level daily about every 15 minutes between 5am and midnight. It takes 35 to 40 minutes to get to Pioneer Courthouse Square in the heart of downtown. To reach destinations in the southeast, northeast, and northwest parts of the city, you can get off at an earlier stop and transfer to a city bus, streetcar, or another MAX line. The adult MAX fare is $2.50 (seniors, or "Honored Citizens," ride for $1.25). For further public transport information, see Getting Around, p 166.

By Car

Portland is 175 miles south of Seattle; 285 miles south of Vancouver, British Columbia; 640 miles north of San Francisco; and 1,015 miles north of Los Angeles, all via **I-5,** the interstate backbone of the West Coast. Starting in Portland, **I-84** runs east to Idaho and Utah.

By Train

Amtrak trains stop at the historic **Union Station,** 800 NW 6th Ave. (☎ 800/872-7245 or 503/273-4860; www.amtrak.com), 12 blocks from Pioneer Courthouse Square. *The Coast Starlight* train from Seattle to Los Angeles stops at Portland, as well as Sacramento, San Francisco, and Santa Barbara. *The Empire Builder* heads east to Chicago via Spokane, St. Paul/Minneapolis, and

Milwaukee. The newer, faster **Amtrak *Cascades*** (www.amtrak cascades.com) train makes the run between Portland and Seattle in 3½ hours (versus 4½ hours for the regular train). The whole Cascades route extends from Eugene, Oregon, to Vancouver, British Columbia.

Taxis are usually waiting outside Union Station, or you **can** arrange a ride through **Uber** or Lyft. The MAX light-rail green and yellow lines stop about a block away at NW 6th Avenue, and Hoyt Street, and bus routes 7, 9, and 33 stop within a block of the station to the south, toward downtown.

By Bus
The **Greyhound Bus Lines** station is at 550 NW 6th Ave. (☎ 800/231-2222 or 503/243-2361; www.greyhound.com), just across NW Irving Street from Union Station. The Union Station/NW 6th & Hoyt Street MAX stop (green and yellow lines) is right outside, as are stops for city bus routes 7, 9, and 33.

Bolt Bus (☎ 877/265-8287; www.boltbus.com) is a super-cheap bus service between Portland, Eugene, Seattle, and Vancouver, BC. Prices vary according to demand. It departs and arrives at SW Salmon Street between 5th and 6th avenues.

Getting **Around**

Portland encourages the use of public transportation, and you can easily travel around the city via bus, MAX light rail, or the Portland Streetcar, all operated by **TriMet** (☎ 503/238-7433; www.trimet.org). The TriMet website is useful for planning trips. Note that the Portland Streetcar has a separate website: www.portlandstreetcar.org.

Navigation
Portland addresses are always tagged with a map quadrant: **NE** (northeast), **SE** (southeast), **SW** (southwest), **NW** (northwest) and **N** (north). The dividing lines are the Willamette River between east and west and Burnside Street between north and south. (Burnside itself is split into "East" and "West" on either side of the river.) All of downtown is SW (southwest). You may find the same street name on both sides of the river, just in different quadrants—say, SW Salmon Street and SE Salmon Street. The only exception is North Portland, a big wedge of the city on the east side of the Willamette between I-5

(to the east) and the river (to the west). Addresses here are simply "North" whatever.

Other navigational quirks: Avenues run north to south and streets run east to west; street names in Northwest Portland are alphabetical heading north from Burnside to Wilson; and on the west side, what would be 7th and 8th avenues are instead named Broadway and Park avenues, respectively.

By Light Rail
Portland's light-rail system, the **Metropolitan Area Express** (MAX), connects downtown with the airport, the eastern suburb of Gresham, the western suburbs of Beaverton and Hillsboro, North Portland, and Milwaukie to the south. Train service begins at 5am and runs until midnight. Note that MAX cars have hooks for hanging bicycles inside.

By Streetcar
The **Portland Streetcar** (www.portlandstreetcar.org) runs a 4-mile NS (north-south) route from the

South Waterfront District through downtown and the Pearl District to NW 23rd and Marshall. The A and B Loops run clockwise and counter-clockwise along a circular 3⅓-mile route, crossing the river via the Broadway Bridge and the Tilikum Crossing bridge (opened in 2015). This route connects downtown with the Moda Center, the Convention Center, the Lloyd District, and OMSI. Streetcars run about every 13 to 20 minutes daily from 5:30am to 11:30pm on weekdays, 7:15am to 11:30pm on Saturday, and 7:15am to 10:30pm on Sunday.

By Bus

TriMet buses operate daily over an extensive network, stretching from Forest Grove to Gresham and from North Portland to Oregon City. Just over half the bus lines run about every 15 minutes during the morning and afternoon rush hours on weekdays. Service is less frequent in the early morning, midday, and evening. Buses run from about 5am to 1 or 2am, depending on the route. Every bus has a rack on the front that can hold two bikes. You can find out when the next bus is arriving at your stop by calling **TriMet** at ☎ 503/238-7433 and entering the ID number posted on the bus stop.

Fares

Fares are the same for MAX and buses: $2.50 for adults, $1.25 for seniors 65 years and older, and $1.50 ages 7 through 17. Streetcar fares are slightly lower: $2 for adults, $1.25 for seniors and youth. A ticket is valid for 2 hours. You can also buy an all-day ticket for $5, which is valid on buses, streetcars, and MAX. Buy tickets or day passes at vending machines at bus, light rail, and streetcar stops, in vending machines on board the streetcar, or at the TriMet Ticket Office, 701 SW Sixth Ave., in Pioneer Courthouse

Square (open Mon–Fri 8:30am–5:30pm, Sat 10am–4pm). You can also buy tickets at most local Albertsons, Fred Meyer, and Safeway grocery stores. If you buy a ticket on the bus, you'll need exact change.

By Car

Oregon drivers still tend to be on the civil side; if you honk your horn in anything but a serious situation, you'll get funny looks (or worse). And don't even try to pump your own gas: Oregon and New Jersey are the only two states where attendants are required to do this for you. It's **illegal to text or talk on a cell-phone** while driving without using a hands-free accessory—and even that's illegal if you're under 18.

You may turn right on a red light after a full stop, and if you are in the far-left lane of a one-way street, you may turn left into the adjacent left lane of a one-way street at a red light after a full stop. Everyone in a moving vehicle is required to wear a seat belt. Drivers must always stop for pedestrians in striped pedestrian crossings.

Portlanders are generally used to driving with bicyclists on the road, but visiting drivers should be extra wary, especially at night and in the rain, because some bikers refuse to use lights or wear helmets. As traffic goes, Portland ranks in the top 20% of cities with bad congestion nationwide. I-5, I-84, and I-205 all often back up during rush hour, when bridges and interchanges turn into chokepoints. The I-5 corridor between Portland and Vancouver, Washington, qualifies as a real traffic nightmare and should be avoided between 8 and 10am and 3 and 7pm.

Many of the blocks in downtown, the Pearl District, and the Lloyd District have electronic SmartMeter pay stations for **street parking.** These take cash and credit cards and spit out parking receipts that you attach to your curbside window. One benefit is that you can use your remaining time at another parking space. You're generally required to pay from 8am to 7pm Monday through Saturday and 1 to 7pm on Sunday, and the rate is $1 to $2 per hour.

The best parking deal in town is the six city-owned **SmartPark garages** (☎ 503/790-9300) downtown with nearly 4,000 public spaces. Four of these are open 24/7. Rates are $1.60 per hour for the first hour and $3 to $5 per hour after that. All-day parking is $12 to $15. You'll find SmartPark garages at 1st Avenue and Jefferson Street, 4th Avenue and Yamhill Street, 10th Avenue and Yamhill Street, 3rd Avenue and Alder Street, O'Bryant Square, Naito Parkway and Davis Street, and Station Place (in the Pearl District near Union Station).

A car is by far the best way to access points outside the city. There just isn't any other way, short of booking a tour, to get to the more remote natural wonders or to fully appreciate such regions as the Oregon coast, Wine Country, or the Columbia River Gorge.

Car-sharing in America was born in Portland in 1998 and has continued to evolve as old car-share companies merge or are bought by other companies. **Car2go** (www. car2go.com) lets you rent a small two-seater car or larger cars (including Mercedes) from spots all over Portland, drive it as long as you need to, and return it to a convenient drop-off spot—not necessarily where you picked it up—for a standard rate of 35-49¢ per minute. You don't have to pay for gas when you use the car. You do need to become a member before you begin using the service, but after the initial charge there is no annual fee. The same basic rules apply for **ReachNow Car**

Sharing Portland (www.reachnow. com/portland), but this service provides various BMW and Mini cars and offers a flat-rate pricing system ($20 for 1 hour, $50 for 3 hours).

By Taxi

Although there are almost always taxis waiting in line at major hotels, you won't find them cruising the streets—you'll have to call ahead for one. **Broadway Cab** (☎ 503/227-1234; www.broadwaycab.com) charges $2.90 per mile and $1 for each additional passenger, with a $2.50 airport pickup surcharge.

Uber (www.uber.com) and **Lyft** (www.lyft.com) ride services are also available in Portland. From the airport, they add a $5 surcharge.

By Bike

With traffic a growing problem in Portland, getting around by bike is an increasingly popular mode of transportation—and now it's easier than ever for you to hop on a bike and pedal to your destination. **BIKETOWN** (**www.biketownpdx.com**), launched in 2016, is Portland's **bikeshare program,** designed for taking quick trips around downtown and the close-in east side. The bright orange bike stations are located in busy areas throughout the Portland core. BIKETOWN offers three payment options: a single 30-minute ride for $2.50, a day pass including 180 minutes of ride time for $12, and an annual pass with 90 minutes of ride time per day for $12/month. The plans are available for purchase through the website, the mobile app, or at a station kiosk. At the station, you enter the pin number you received with sign-up or hold your member card above the touch pad, remove the lock, ride the bike, and return it to an open space at any other bike station. It's fun and simple.

A progressive citywide bike transportation program includes ubiquitous bike racks on buses and the light-rail (MAX), and wide, clear bike lanes on most major commuter routes. Riders are required to obey all traffic laws—cops give out real tickets for not coming to a full stop at stop signs, for instance—and you have to give pedestrians right-of-way on sidewalks (obviously). For more information and news about biking in Portland, check out **BikePortland** (www.bikeportland.org).

Fast **Facts**

AREA CODE The area code for most of Portland is **503**, with **971** as the new additional code. For the rest of Oregon, the area codes are **541** and **458.**

BUSINESS HOURS In general, stores are open weekdays 9 or 10am to 5 or 6pm, and Sunday noon to 5pm. Malls typically stay open to 9pm Monday to Saturday. Banks are open Monday to Friday 9am to 5pm (occasionally Sat 9am–noon). Bars and clubs can stay open until 2am.

CANNABIS LAWS since 2015 the recreational use of marijuana has been legal in Portland. You must be 21 years of age to purchase pot from a licensed retailer. Smoking marijuana in public in Oregon is illegal, even if you're smoking with a vape pen. You can only consume at home or on private property—but not in your hotel. This means no bars, community parks, public outdoor smoking areas, on buses and airplanes, or federal land. And don't smoke in your car and then drive when you're stoned: Getting busted for smoking weed in public can result in fines or even jail time.

DENTIST Contact the **Multnomah Dental Society** (☎ 503/513-5010; www.multnomahdental.org) for a referral.

DISABLED TRAVELERS Wheelchair users will find most of the city relatively flat, outside of the West Hills and Mount Tabor. Buses, MAX light-rail, and the Portland Streetcar are all equipped with lifts for wheelchairs. Most hotels provide wheelchair-accessible rooms, and some of the larger and more expensive hotels also have TDD telephones and other amenities for the hearing- and sight-impaired. Sidewalk ramps are the norm downtown but are more randomly placed elsewhere. Organizations that offer resources and assistance to travelers with disabilities include the **American Foundation for the Blind** (☎ 800/232-5463; www.afb. org); and the **Society for Accessible Travel & Hospitality** (☎ 212/447-7284; www.sath.org).

DOCTORS See "Hospitals," below.

DRINKING LAWS The legal minimum drinking age in Oregon is 21. Beer and wine are available in grocery stores and convenience stores, and hard liquor can be purchased in bars, restaurants, and liquor stores. Brewpubs tend to sell only beer and wine, but some also have hard liquor licenses.

ELECTRICITY The U.S. uses 110–120 volts AC (60 cycles). You'll need a 110-volt transformer and a plug adapter with two flat parallel pins to use 220–240 volt appliances. (It's best to bring one from home.)

EMBASSIES & CONSULATES All embassies are in the U.S. capital, Washington, D.C. There are also consulates in some major U.S. cities, though none are in Portland.

Most nations also have a mission to the United Nations in New York City. If your country isn't listed below, call for directory information in Washington, D.C. (☎ 202/555-1212) or check www.embassy.org/embassies.

The embassy of **Australia** is at 1601 Massachusetts Ave. NW, Washington, D.C. 20036 (☎ 202/797-3000; www.usa.embassy.gov.au). Consulates are in New York, Honolulu, Houston, Los Angeles, and San Francisco.

The embassy of **Canada** is at 501 Pennsylvania Ave. NW, Washington, D.C. 20001 (☎ 202/682-1740; www.can-am.gc.ca/washington). Canadian consulates are in Buffalo (New York), Detroit, Los Angeles, New York, and Seattle.

The embassy of **Ireland** is at 2234 Massachusetts Ave. NW, Washington, D.C. 20008 (☎ 202/462-3939; www.embassyofireland.org). Irish consulates are in Boston, Chicago, New York, San Francisco, and other cities. See website for complete listing.

The embassy of **New Zealand** is at 37 Observatory Circle NW, Washington, D.C. 20008 (☎ 202/328-4800; www.nzembassy.com). New Zealand consulates are in Los Angeles, Salt Lake City, San Francisco, and Seattle.

The embassy of the **United Kingdom** is at 3100 Massachusetts Ave. NW, Washington, D.C. 20008 (☎ 202/588-6500; http://ukinusa.fco.gov.uk). Other British consulates are in Atlanta, Boston, Chicago, Cleveland, Houston, Los Angeles, New York, San Francisco, and Seattle.

EMERGENCIES Dial **911** for fire, police, and medical emergencies.

HOLIDAYS Government offices, post offices, banks, and many restaurants, stores, and museums are closed on the following national

holidays: January 1 (New Year's Day), the third Monday in January (Martin Luther King, Jr. Day), the third Monday in February (Presidents' Day), the last Monday in May (Memorial Day), July 4 (Independence Day), the first Monday in September (Labor Day), the second Monday in October (Columbus Day), November 11 (Veterans Day), the fourth Thursday in November (Thanksgiving Day), and December 25 (Christmas). Banks and offices may also be closed on Election Day, which (in election years) is the Tuesday after the first Monday in November.

HOSPITALS Hospitals convenient to downtown include **Oregon Health & Science University,** 3181 SW Sam Jackson Park Rd. (☎ 503/494-8311; www.ohsu.edu), **Providence Portland Medical Center,** 4805 NE Glisan St. (☎ 503/574-6595; http://oregon.providence.org), and **Legacy Good Samaritan,** 1015 NW 22nd Ave. (☎ 503/413-7711; www.legacyhealth.org). Legacy has a physician referral service at ☎ 503/335-3500.

INSURANCE For information on traveler's insurance, trip cancelation insurance, and medical insurance while traveling, please visit www.frommers.com/planning.

INTERNET & WI-FI Most of Portland's coffee shops offer free Wi-Fi, as do the branches of the **Multnomah County Library** (☎ 503/988-5402; www.multcolib.org), which also have Internet terminals available to all. Most hotels offer free Internet access as well.

LEGAL AID While driving, if you are pulled over for a minor infraction (such as speeding), never attempt to pay the fine directly to a police officer; this could be construed as attempted bribery, a much more serious crime. Pay fines by mail, or directly into the hands of the clerk of the court. If accused of a more serious offense, say and do nothing before consulting a lawyer. In the U.S., the burden is on the state to prove a person's guilt beyond a reasonable doubt, and everyone has the right to remain silent, whether he or she is suspected of a crime or actually arrested. Once arrested, a person can make one telephone call to a party of his or her choice. The international visitor should call his or her embassy or consulate.

LGBT TRAVELERS Though it has seen more than its share of anti-gay rights battles, Portland has always been a fairly tolerant city. Same-sex couples have been able to marry in Oregon since 2014.To find out what's going on in the LGBT community, pick up a free copy of the bimonthly *Just Out* (☎ 503/236-1252; www.justout.com). The **Gay & Lesbian Community Yellow Pages** (☎ 503/230-7701; www.pdxgay yellowpages.com) lists gay-owned and gay-friendly businesses. Also check with Portland's **LGBT Q Center** (www.pdxqcenter.org).

MAIL The main post office in Portland is at 715 NW Hoyt St. (☎ 800/ASK-USPS or 503/525-5398; www.usps.com). It's open Monday through Friday from 8am to 6:30pm, Saturday from 8:30am to 5pm.

NEWSPAPERS & MAGAZINES The *Oregonian* (www.oregonlive.com) is Portland's major newspaper, followed by *Portland Tribune*. The *Portland Mercury* (www.portland-mercury.com) and *Willamette Week* (www.wweek.com) are free weekly arts and entertainment newspapers.

PASSPORTS Virtually every air traveler entering the U.S. is required to show a passport.

For Residents of Australia: Call Australian Passport Information Service (☎ 131-232, or visit www. passports.gov.au).

For Residents of Canada: Passport Office, Department of Foreign Affairs and International Trade, Ottawa, ON K1A 0G3 (☎ 800/567-6868; www.ppt.gc.ca).

For Residents of Ireland: Passport Office, Setanta Centre, Molesworth St., Dublin 2 (☎ 01/671-1633; www.foreignaffairs.gov.ie).

For Residents of New Zealand: Passports Office, Department of Internal Affairs, 47 Boulcott St., Wellington, 6011 (☎ 0800/225-050 in New Zealand or 04/474-8100; www.passports.govt.nz).

For **Residents of the United Kingdom:** Visit your nearest passport office, major post office, or travel agency or contact the Identity and Passport Service (IPS), 89 Eccleston Square, London, SW1V 1PN (☎ 0300/222-0000; www.ips.gov.uk).

PHARMACIES Conveniently located downtown pharmacies include **Rite Aid,** 622 SW Alder St. (☎ 503/226-6791), which is open weekdays 7am to 11pm, and **Central Drug,** 538 SW 4th Ave. (☎ 503/226-2222). Fred Meyer and Safeway grocery stores have pharmacies as well.

POLICE The **Portland Police Bureau**'s central precinct is at 1111 SW 2nd Ave. (☎ 503/823-0000; www.portlandpolice.com). Dial **911** for emergencies.

SAFETY Portland is a relatively safe city, but you should take some precautions if you're visiting the Chinatown and Old Town districts at night. Don't leave anything valuable in your car while you're hiking in Forest Park. As a general rule, avoid deserted areas, especially at night, and don't go into public parks at night. Park in well-lit, busy areas whenever possible.

SMOKING Smoking is banned in public indoor spaces throughout the state of Oregon, even bars, as well as within 10 feet of entrances, exits, and windows.

TAXES Oregon is one of only five states with no sales tax, making it a shopper's delight. In Portland, there are 12.5% taxes on both hotel rooms and car rentals (plus an additional fee of 10%–15% if you pick up your rental car at the airport).

TIME Portland is on Pacific time, 3 hours behind Eastern Standard Time, and 8 hours behind Greenwich Mean Time. In the summer, daylight saving time is observed and clocks are set forward 1 hour.

TIPPING Waiters generally receive 15%–20% of the bill; taxi drivers 15% of fare; bartenders $1 per drink; hotel chamber staff $1–$2 per day; skycaps and valets $1–$2 per bag; and valet parking attendants $1 per ride.

TOILETS Portland may be the only city with its own patented public toilet, the **Portland Loo** (www. portlandloo.com). Find these solar-powered, 24-hour restrooms along SW Naito Parkway in Waterfront Park at both SW Ash and SW Taylor streets, as well as at NW Glisan Street between SW 5th and 6th avenues, and at Jamison Square at NW Johnson Street and NW 11th Avenue. Otherwise, look for restrooms in most Starbucks and hotel lobbies.

VISAS The U.S. State Department has a **Visa Waiver Program (VWP)** allowing citizens of the following countries to enter the United States without a visa for stays of up to 90 days: Andorra, Australia, Austria, Belgium, Brunei, Czech Republic, Denmark, Estonia, Finland, France, Germany, Greece, Hungary,

Iceland, Ireland, Italy, Japan, Latvia, Liechtenstein, Lithuania, Luxembourg, Malta, Monaco, the Netherlands, New Zealand, Norway, Portugal, San Marino, Singapore, Slovakia, Slovenia, South Korea, Spain, Sweden, Switzerland, and the United Kingdom. (**Note:** This list was accurate at press time; for the most up-to-date list of countries in the VWP, consult www.dhs. gov/visa-waiver-program.) Even though a visa isn't necessary for citizens of those countries, in an effort to help U.S. officials check travelers against terror watch lists before they arrive at U.S. borders, visitors from VWP countries must register online through the **Electronic System for Travel Authorization (ESTA)** before boarding a plane or a boat to the U.S. Travelers must complete an electronic application providing basic personal and travel eligibility information. The Department of Homeland Security recommends filling out the form at least 3 days before traveling. Authorizations will be valid for up to 2 years or until the traveler's passport expires, whichever comes first. Currently, there is a US$14 fee for the online application. For more information, go to www.dhs.gov/visa-waiver-program. **Canadian citizens** may enter the United States without visas, but will need to show passports and proof of residence.

Citizens of all other countries must have (1) a valid passport that expires at least 6 months later than the scheduled end of their visit to the U.S.; and (2) a tourist visa.

Portland: **A Brief History**

15,000–13,000 B.C. Cataclysmic floods carve the Columbia Gorge, with waters reaching as high as Crown Point.

12,300 B.C. Earliest known human inhabitants in Oregon, near Paisley, 220 miles southeast of Eugene.

1579 English explorer Sir Francis Drake reaches the mouth of the Rogue River in southwest Oregon, turned back by "thicke and stinking fogges."

1792 American captain Robert Gray becomes first to sail into the Columbia River, names it in honor of his ship the *Columbia Rediviva*.

1805 Expedition led by Meriwether Lewis and William Clark reaches the Pacific Ocean at the mouth of the Columbia River, and spends a miserable winter in Fort Clatsop.

1824 Fort Vancouver, fur-trading outpost of the Hudson's Bay Company, founded across the Columbia River from present-day Portland.

1841 Bartleson-Bidwell Party, the first group to make a wagon crossing of the Oregon Trail, reaches the Willamette Valley from Missouri.

1843 Business partners Asa Lovejoy and William Overton pay 25¢ filing fee to claim 640 acres on the west bank of the Willamette River in present-day Portland; settlers elect provisional government.

1844 Oregon City becomes first incorporated town west of the Rocky Mountains.

1845 Asa Lovejoy and new partner Francis Pettygrove flip a coin to name the settlement called simply "The Clearing"; Pettygrove wins and names it after his hometown of Portland, Maine.

1840S–1860S About 400,000 emigrants travel west on the Oregon Trail.

1848 Oregon becomes first U.S. territory west of the Rockies; Pettygrove sells nearly the entire townsite of Portland to tanner Daniel Lownsdale for $5,000 worth of leather, despite only owning half of it.

1851 City of Portland incorporated.

1879 First telephone lines installed.

1880 First electric street lights arrive.

1883 Northern Pacific Railroad reaches Portland.

1888 Steel Bridge #1 opens, the first steel bridge on the West Coast.

1889 Local newspapers call Portland "the most filthy city in the Northern States" with sidewalks that would be a "disgrace to a Russian village."

1905 Lewis and Clark Centennial Exposition held, including the Forestry Building, "the world's greatest log cabin."

1907 Oaks Amusement Park opens; first Rose Festival held.

1908 Portland Police Department hires Lola Greene Baldwin, the nation's first policewoman.

1915 Columbia River Gorge scenic highway constructed.

1917 International Rose Test Garden established.

1940S Portland's Kaiser shipyards become the world's leading shipbuilders due to the war effort. Portland becomes a boomtown as tens of thousands of workers, including the first African-Americans, flock to Portland for war-related work, while Japanese-Americans in Portland and throughout the West Coast are sent to internment camps for the duration of the war.

1946 Portland State University founded.

1948 A dike holding back the Columbia River collapses and floodwaters destroy the hastily constructed public housing community known as Vanport, built in north Portland for war-industry workers; 15 are killed.

LATE 1940S–1950S Organized crime, corruption, and vice dominate local politics, resulting in indictments of the Multnomah county district attorney and Portland's mayor and chief of police. In 1949, Dorothy McCullough Lee is elected the first female mayor of Portland and promises to rid the city of gambling, corruption, and prostitution.

1957 Elvis Presley performs in front of 14,000 people at Multnomah Stadium (now Providence Park), one of the first outdoor stadium rock concerts.

1960S Winemakers plant Oregon's first pinot noir vines in the Umpqua Valley, southwest of Eugene, starting modern era of Oregon winemaking.

1964 Nike founded by University of Oregon track runner Philip Knight and coach Bill Bowerman.

1965 The Beatles play two shows at Memorial Coliseum for 20,000 fans, inspiring Allen Ginsberg's poem "Portland Coliseum."

1974 Harbor Drive freeway along downtown waterfront is removed, eventually to be replaced with Waterfront Park.

1977 Portland Trail Blazers win NBA Championship for the first and only time (so far).

1980S–1990S Portland is roiled by several costly and virulent anti-gay rights battles.

1980 Mt. St. Helens erupts, killing 57 people and blanketing Portland in ash.

1985 First light rail train route opens; *Portlandia* statue installed.

1990S Dot-com boom brings an influx of artists, graphic designers, and Internet entrepreneurs to Portland; dot-com bust brings even more from Seattle and San Francisco.

1993 Vera Katz is elected 49th mayor of Portland and serves until 2005; she is widely considered to be one of Portland's most effective mayors.

1998 Oregon becomes the first state to legalize euthanasia with the Death with Dignity Act.

2001 Portland becomes first city in the U.S. to (re-)introduce modern streetcar service.

2004 Multnomah County starts issuing marriage license to same-sex couples. Over 3,000 gay couples rush to get married.

2005 After a court challenge and public referendum, Multnomah County rescinds same-sex marriage and invalidates all same-sex marriages.

2008 Oregon Legislature passes the Family Fairness Act, allowing same-sex couple to establish domestic partnerships.

2010 *Portlandia* comedy series premieres on IFC, poking fun at the city "where young people go to retire."

2014 Oregon becomes the 15th state to strike down discriminatory marriage laws, making it legal for same-sex couples to wed.

Portland Reads

Portland has long been a magnet for writers and the readers who love them. There's a long list of books by local authors, about Portland, or both. Here are a few classics:

- Swan Adamson, *My Three Husbands* and *Memoirs Are Made of This*
- Jean M. Auel, *The Clan of the Cave Bear*
- Beverly Cleary, *Ramona the Pest*
- Katherine Dunn, *Geek Love*
- Stewart Holbrook, *The Portland Story*
- Ursula K. Le Guin, *The Lathe of Heaven*
- Donald Olson, *The Pacific Northwest Garden Tour*
- Chuck Palahniuk, *Fugitives and Refugees: A Walk in Portland, Oregon*
- Joe Sacco, *Palestine*

2015 Oregon legalizes growing and possession of small amounts of marijuana for recreational use; pot boutiques open in Portland.

2014–2018 Portland grows at a phenomenal rate, resulting in a citywide building boom, soaring rents, and traffic congestion.

2017 Two men are fatally stabbed on a MAX train when they try to stop a white-supremacist from spewing racial epithets at two women wearing headscarves. Summer forest fires in the Columbia Gorge and southern Oregon burn more than 150,000 acres and blanket the region with smoke that makes the air quality in Portland the worst in the country. Sixth and final season of TV series *Portlandia* airs.

Index

See also Accommodations and Restaurant indexes, below.

Accommodations Index

Photo **Credits**

Notes

MC OCT 2018